SUCCESS WITH PIKE

SUCCESS WITH
PIKE

BARRIE RICKARDS
WITH
COLIN DYSON AND MARTIN GAY

David & Charles

A catalogue record for this book is available from the British
Library.

ISBN 0 7153 9932 2

Typeset by ICON, Exeter
and printed in Great Britain by Redwood Press Ltd
for David & Charles
Brunel House Newton Abbot Devon

CONTENTS

Barrie Rickards

A PHILOSOPHY OF SUCCESS

Success comes in two forms: that which is a personal success for the individual; and that which is measurably a success by some arbitrary standard, such as national guidelines quality of catches. Both are legitimate targets for an angler and in this book we set down the techniques and philosophies which lead to success of either kind. Some pursue only personal success or catch improvement, and it is certainly easier to equate such success with enjoyment of a relaxing kind. For these anglers it is not essential to visit the 'going' water of the day and, fish with the crowds. On the other hand, plenty of successful pike anglers do just that. For them it is easier to measure their success against a yardstick of national standards, even though it is artificial and everchanging. I cannot speak for my fellow contributors to this book, but I am more of the first category, even though my own catches do withstand national scrutiny of a close kind. I am far from opposed to those who chase from water to water, and I do not make the error of thinking that they all seek some kind of national glory or recognition: plenty of them simply want to catch a real monster. I have done enough of this kind of fishing in my younger years not to wish to do it now – but I do not decry it, and at intervals in this text clear guidance will be given as to how to pursue that goal.

It is obvious that one definition of successful angling is an enjoyable day at the waterside. For me this may or may not include the company of individuals, and both the water and the catch may be quite varied. On some of the more remote waters that I fish, a pike of 20lb is unusual, but my memories of those places are the beauty of the waters, the company perhaps, the learning process, and the pike caught as well. I must have a chance of pike, perhaps in quality or quantity, or there must be an exploratory factor, something of the unknown to aid the learning process. It is possible to fish quiet waters, small waters, varied waters, and to catch fish to the national standards. Not all waters are heavily fished or fished out, and unless there is an unprecedented increase in the number of pike anglers, they never will be. It will always be possible to explore and to discover.

In Chapter 8 I draw attention to the fact that the innovators of pike tackle

Barrie Rickards instructing youngsters in the skills of lure fishing on a Cambridge City Council angling course run by BR and Percy Anderson (standing)

or technique have not usually been the camp followers: that is the only real drawback to chasing big fish from known waters. Quite simply, it may not be rewarding enough for the intelligent mind – the fish are there, because someone else has proved it and it may simply be a matter of time, of waiting, until you catch *your* big fish. It *may* have been caught previously, of course, and you *may* learn nothing about catching pike to help you the next time, on another water. Some of these worries can be avoided by fishing the really big waters, like Loch Lomond (see Chapters 4 and 5). And we have extensive sections in this tome telling you how to tackle the big waters. These are followed by Chapter 7 which explains the principles of going it alone and 'Cracking a New Water'. Before that all in the way of tackle and techniques will have been laid bare.

I cannot easily measure all the aspects of my own success, because they are tied up with imponderables of philosophy, of unquantifiable experiences. The catches are measurable enough. At the end of the 1990–1 season, I had taken 1,349 pike over 10lb. I have no summary record of how many waters they came from, but it is a very large number from all over these islands, and of all types of water from tiny stream to giant loch. I have only once caught less than 25 double-figure fish in a season, and that was in the 1974–5 season when I had 23. Only once have I exceeded 100 fish, and that was in 1988–9 when I took 110 such fish. The average catch per annum in recent years has been about 75; in the 1960s and early 1970s it was nearer 45.

I have caught 128 pike over 20lb, from 23 different waters. A few of them are repeat captures, but only a few. One fish I have caught three times. Others I may not know about. I have caught two fish of 30lb, the best being a whisker over 32lb, a river fish. This last was 47½in long and could, under certain circumstances, have weighed as much as 42lb rather than 32lb.

These fish have fallen to a variety of bait methods and lure fishing. I will detail aspects of the latter in the appropriate chapter, but will here make only two relevant points: of the last 24 twenty-pounders, 14 have fallen to lures, and that in the last two and a half years; my greatest ever catch of pike fell to spoon, and in one and a half days' fishing I had 80 pike for a weight in excess of 800lb. The second (full) day's catch was 54 fish for 550lb, with one twenty-pounder and 15 double-figure fish. With 7 doubles the day before, I had a total of 22 doubles in a day and a half! The average weight per fish was 10lb.

I am uncertain of the total number of pike that I have caught, but is somewhere between ten and fifteen thousand, possibly nearer the former. I could under no circumstances consider four or five fish in a season as success, even if they were larger than usual. However, some anglers tolerate this quality of fishing. They know that if they stick at a water long enough, one known to have a few big fish, eventually they will catch if their bait is in the water long enough. This approach is anathema to me. It is failure, not success. A couple of years ago one of my close colleagues, Tim Cole, and I, visited a water where that kind of fishing was what the local pike anglers had come to expect. The water was overfished and it was hard to find a swim that was not occupied by a bivvy. Our advice was that they should leave the place immediately and find other waters, new and unfished. We drove home that night and resolved to keep a record, the coming season, of every single pike we caught, in an attempt to put things into perspective, to show what could be done with initiative. That was the 1988–9 season, and between us we had 635 pike – 358 to me and 277 to Tim (who fished less frequently). In fact, including the catches of a few additional friends, we had over 2,500 pike during 1987–9. These fish came from more than forty waters, of all kinds, and from several different counties. Of the 635, 132 were in double figures and 11 were twenty-pounders. The average weight of all the fish was 9¼lb. Between four and ten runs in a season is abject failure: 635 fish is success. And being successful is what this book is about.

I also demand certain standards of myself and of others. I detest despoilers of the countryside. I dislike anglers who not behave properly with respect to the pike's well-being. When I used to fish Ardingly in Sussex, I met a nice stamp of angler, even when we were all fishing in a line on the bank, 20yd apart. At other crowded venues I would feel uneasy about turning my back on my brolly camp. There are standards of behaviour to other anglers, other countryside users and to fish, which seem to get swamped at times under the ever-increasing tide of pikers. I am optimistic, by and large, that we can cope with the increase, but only if those experienced anglers, through such organisations as the Pike Anglers' Club of Great Britain, actually *set* standards and pass them on to new pikers. In that way we shall all enjoy success with common sense, rather than success at any cost.

1

THE LORE
OF THE PIKE

If you are of the opinion, which I think stems from mythology, that pike are the lone wolves of freshwater and that you should hunt them as such, then you will catch few pike. Perhaps you will catch the sprinkling of fish that you deserve. Pike lore has it that the species behaves like the lone wolf, waiting in ambush. However the analogy is rather poor, because wolves are unusual, rather they hunt in packs and roam far and wide. When pike do roam, on the hunt, they probably do not do so as a pack but when they sit quietly, waiting opportunist fashion for food to come to them, then they group together. There is no ready analogy with wolf behaviour.

Such an analogy arose because when man first encountered pike in the cool part of the Northern Hemisphere, at about the time of the Ice Age, the wolf was the main predator known to him. Had the pike and man coincided in more southerly climes, the analogy might have been made with lion prides, and there would have been a better analogy by far, as I shall explain below.

I do feel very strongly that history has determined what we feel about the pike and because science in history is often very wrong then what we feel about the role of pike is often very wrong too.

Opinion about the role of the pike is not, or was not, based upon observation and deduction, but upon fear and superstition. It was believed that pike pulled in horses by grabbing their muzzles as they drank; that they bred from pickerel weed, unlike other creatures. Aspects of these misconceptions still survive, such as the belief that pike grow to a weight of 90lb, and the oft-repeated stories (in the press) that they regularly eat ducks. However, although this is an interesting subject which is at long last being studied, I shall not dwell further on it in the body of the book.

PIKE ACTIVITY BEFORE SPAWNING TIME

To have real success with pike it is important to understand how they feed. For a long time it has been known that pike gather in groups at spawning time, and that they may move a considerable distance to a preferred spawning site. I fish one river where the spawning site is the junction with a side stream. The main river itself has little to distinguish one section from another, but it is slightly wider where the side stream joins, and the whole water is shallow and a uniform depth of 4ft. The fish spawn in the river itself, not the side stream, and there is no clear reason why they should choose that place, unless perhaps the deposited eggs get a fresh flush of water over them at intervals. This is unlikely as it happens. Be that as it may, in the last two weeks of the season – 1–14 March – the angler should be seated in that place because the big females will arrive there sooner or later.

Several miles away on the same river the spawning grounds are about a hundred yards of shallow water, about 1ft deep, on either side of which the water drops to its normal 4ft depth. So it is clear that big or long waters may have several spawning sites, and that those spawning sites may have, therefore, a catchment area. In the first case, the big big females are never far away, certainly within 2 miles either side of the site for spawning; the males, however, may roam more widely.

The question for the angler is when he should begin his wait for the big fish to arrive. If he starts too early, say January or the first half of February, then he may catch little at first. Then the smaller males will arrive on the site. Small males – and they rarely reach 10lb – make a habit of avoiding females simply because they get eaten, regularly. Some years, by the end of January, the females will arrive on the site, or be nearby, perhaps a hundred yards or so away, or just over the drop-off if there is one.

I'm uneasy in my mind about the crucial factor in pike spawning. It is generally accepted that pike spawning is temperature controlled, and that in a mild winter the pike will spawn earlier. I can think of several instances when mild spells at the end of the season have had the pike actually spawning, or spawned, in early March. Normally, in an average winter, they probably spawn just after the fishing season, in mid-March. What worries me is that in the 1963 freeze-up the pike certainly spawned in early March, beneath the ice, because I caught several post-spawning fish, as the ice thawed rapidly in the last three days of the season. However, this was a chalk stream and apart from the skin of ice on the top it may have been at a very constant low temperature which the pike were used to. On the other hand, it may be that pike spawn when they sense that the weather is about to come right for the eggs and fry to have a chance.

Temperature certainly affects the rate at which the eggs hatch. For example, at 'normal' temperatures in March, the eggs hatch in about two weeks. But at higher temperatures, of the mid-60s (°F), they will hatch in four or five days. If there is an optimum incubation period, then there could be a preferred temperature range for spawning.

As predators of pike, anglers need to recognise the spawning grounds to give ourselves the chance of a heavy back-end fish or a big bag of fish. However, there is another factor we can exploit. In order to reach the spawning sites the pike have to travel there. If you identify the travel route, you will have a chance of intercepting them. Perhaps more importantly, if you identify the *rate* of travel, you will be able to stay with them once located, bearing in mind, of course, that pike locked into spawning mode will probably not remain in the same place when they are returned, but simply continue where they left off, moving slowly towards their goal of the spawning site.

In the case of the first spawning site that I mentioned earlier, the approaching pike seemed to travel at about one hundred yards or so each week. However, this was fairly close to the site and they may have been slowing down, waiting in the area for the trigger to set them off. If they travel at this speed all the time, it would take them four months to cover a mile – that is, they would start in early December to cover the last mile. This I do not think is the case, for the big females are static, and grouped, for other reasons, certainly up to and including December. I think that they may start their migration for spawning in January, moving fairly quickly at first once the urge has begun, and then slowing down as the site is approached. Certainly January is an odd month for piking and pike do turn up where you least expect them. The smaller males – jack pike – may well arrive on the spawning beds more than two weeks before the females. The big females know they are there and the odd big marauder may arrive in an attempt to mop up a few, and then move away again.

Each water must have different spawning migration rates, routes and timing. In small waters, which often have a few big pike, the spawners may need to travel less than a hundred yards to reach their destination. Nevertheless, recognise the movement and the time of it, and you may well see a giant fish that you did not know was in the water.

CANNIBALISM

After spawning, the jack pike hightail it as far and fast as they can go to get away from the females. They look for the emerging weed growth as cover, and man-made holts. *They* do not stay in groups but seek safety in a hideaway site, on their own. So jack pike would have helped to maintain the myth of the lone wolf. A few of them may stay on the spawning site, because once the pike fry are around there will be good feeding. However, a small number of females will stay in the area too, so that decision is a risky one. Remember that a big pike can always outpace and outmanoeuvre a small pike. One of the prime spawning sites on Loch Lomond, at Ardlui, always had a few big females in residence throughout the summer, as well as larger numbers of jacks.

The fry themselves do not stay long at the spawning site. Once they reach about 4–6oz they begin to spread out because they need the fry shoals of other species to feed on. They probably follow the fry shoals around the weeded, warmer margins. I have witnessed this activity in detail on two quite different waters, one a gravel pit at Waterbeach in Cambridgeshire and one a Fenland Drain in Norfolk. By July numerous jack pike of $^1/_2$–$^3/_4$lb are found all around the margins, often in numbers that make them a nuisance to bottom fishermen. From egg to $^3/_4$lb weight in five months is a reasonable growth rate; sometimes it is much higher than that. By early September the majority of those fish have been eaten. The bigger pike certainly use them as a major food source. It's likely that fish, much fewer in number, weighing around 5–7lb are the culprits. These are the survivors from the previous one or two years' pogroms! It may also be that one or two of the big females stay hooked into pike-eating mode and simply continue in that way.

Such big fish may escape the attention of anglers for a long time, because we do not offer them the food they are eating. Anglers who do use pike as baits report an astonishingly high average size of pike captured – mid-20lb as a rule. When I have tried it myself I have caught those in the 5–7lb bracket! Furthermore, pike-eaters may stay loners, because there is little doubt that the bulk of big pike do not chase smaller pike as a prime food source, although they will eat them readily enough if they do not have to work for them. Occasionally all the pike on a water seem to hook into pike feeding. This is probably when there has been an unusual upsurge of jack pike in the population. I have experienced this now on several waters. The hallmarks are the same each time: the big pike which were being caught go off the feed or 'disappear'; pike that are caught are often much smaller and may be severely damaged, especially at the back end (they have, in fact, escaped murderous assault).

This activity may continue for two or three seasons. The anglers' chances with the big fish are very low, because having eaten pike of 5–8lb weight, the female will rest for a few days, at least, in order to digest her meal. Should an angler be fortunate enough to have one take his 'ordinary' bait, the pike will turn out to be a very fast fighter, in good condition generally, but *empty*! Sometimes such fish have clusters of leeches hanging on their fins where they have remained static near the bottom for long periods.

THE LAIR THEORY AND HOTSPOTS

In the second edition of *Fishing for Big Pike* (1976) I included a slight detraction of my hotspot concept, because the idea had already been outlined by Peter Wheat in 1969 when he detected genuine hotspots on the Hampshire Avon. I think it is fair to say, however, that my Hotspot and Lair Theory was a

Do not dismiss small waters like this one in Fenland (Wicken Fen). In the Fens all waters of this size have pike of 20lb in them

more general case and more widely analysed. As far as I can recall from my reading the word 'hotspot' had never appeared in the literature before Peter Wheat used it. It was very clearly defined by myself in 1971. Since then, however, it has been grossly abused as a term and now seems to apply where anyone catches a fish, whether pike or not.

But that is not so important as understanding what exactly this grouping is – perhaps the Lair Theory is a suitable alternative title. There is no doubt from my experience that on most waters the big fish are grouped closely together, possibly just for their own company, and that this grouping exists through most of the summer, the whole of the autumn, and at least until and including December. It is nothing to do with spawning, but essentially occupies their time for the rest of the year.

In the first instance, the group feeds on any individual or shoal which is unwise enough to wander into the vicinity of a lair. There are no jack pike anywhere near a big pike lair. A peculiarity of this feeding is that it happens at set times of the day (see pp16–17).

Secondly, and rather infrequently, the group moves out far and wide and feeds madly. This event is short-lived – one day – and it may be triggered in the first instance by some activity of food shoals or by weather conditions. But most of the time the group of females is in the lair or hotspot.

The hotspot might be very small; indeed, it usually is. When Ray Webb and I had our first inkling of hotspots we found that the pike on the whole of Hornsea Mere – one of the biggest waters in the country – were located in an area 30yd by 10yd. It sounds fantastic. It sounded so at the time and nobody believed us; but the facts proved it conclusively. For several seasons all the big pike were caught there, despite the fact that many more boats of pikers fished outside the hotspot than in it. The hallmark of a hotspot is that very few big fish are caught outside it except on those occasional days that I have just referred to. Anglers involved in such fishing will deny the facts vehemently, but they catch few fish and simply will not accept the cause.

One hotspot I discovered was a very long cast from the bank, all of seventy yards. An angler I was fishing with refused to try to get the distance, arguing that the idea was a figment of my imagination. My imagination got me fifteen 20lb pike, whereas he caught not one while he fished the same swims with me; nor, indeed, while he fished any other swims.

Hotspots will last for many years, unchanging, unless they are subjected to excessive angling pressure. I have been fishing one now for thirteen years and is is still producing twenty-pounders and a majority of the big fish. Fairly heavy fishing will break up a hotspot; when this happens the group of females probably drifts away, while staying together. There are indications that on some waters the hotspot of pike is not so much the physical location but the biological grouping; it is the group itself that moves around. This is especially so when the water has a large number of features on it – for example, a fea-tureless Fenland drain or river may have a fixed hotspot for decades, or a gravel pit may have a shifting group, albeit one that shifts slowly.

One of the behaviour patterns of pike which turns people off the very idea of hotspots is the returned fish which turns up miles away. Of course, equally often or more often, a returned fish turns up on site. And a returned fish is not a 'normal' fish anyway – it may well go on walk-about for a while after it has been disturbed; or it may have been caught when it was on a feeding spree.

If you find the hotspot or lair or grouping, you will have found success. Pike will feed if you find them first. Let me return now to the feeding patterns themselves. When in their lair pike will feed on most days at a more or less set time. Therefore, if you have found them – and this may be very difficult on some waters – you will get big fish. The feeding time/pattern usually lasts for an hour or so at most, and the actual time may be maintaind for a few days or a few weeks. Often it switches very suddenly and you may feel that the pike have gone. I remember once getting it into my head that the big fish only fed in the early morning. Suddenly they stopped and I assumed that they had gone. However, by chance I dropped in for an afternoon session (previously I'd been going elsewhere at lunchtime!) and there they were.

I do not pretend to know why big females group in this way, nor why they have the feeding patterns that they do. It is possible that the feeding periods are set off by the passage of shoal fish such as roach and bream. Such cyprinid shoals do follow regular migration routes on a daily basis, and they then switch the timing suddenly, but may use part of the same route. So this fits well. It also fits in another sense for I have never subscribed to the view that packs of big pike follow the prey shoals around. Rather, they sit in wait for them, as a general rule. I can imagine that when the prey shoals are in vast numbers and on a *seasonal* migration – for example, with trout runs, salmon parr migration, powan migration etc – then the pike packs will move into close attendance, or ambush. But that is the equivalent of the feeding sprees that I dealt with earlier; it is a relatively short-lived break away from the norm, which is the sit-and-wait-for-it policy.

In summary then, we need to know the how, when and where of the spawning migration, and we need to know the sites of the post-spawning hotspots, more especially in the autumn when the weed growth fails. Alternatively we can roam far and wide fishing for the widely distributed jacks, the occasional lone female, or hope to fish on the days when all the big pike are out on a spree. The choice is ours.

FEEDING HABITS

Another aspect of pike lore that needs to be understood concerns the detail of how they feed, what they feed on, and how their metabolism works, because this fundamentally controls the tackle and techniques.

Pike eat fish. Unlike other species in freshwater they are almost exclusively fish-eaters. Use a rat or a bird, you could well fish for your lifetime without catching a pike – so beware those stories of duck-eating pike! Present your fish bait well, or your imitation of it, and you will succeed sooner or later.

The senses that the pike uses to hunt are important in this context. First, they have unusually good eyesight. Second, they have a strong sense of smell – despite idiotic claims from the Continent that they cannot smell. Third, they can detect vibrations, enabling them to feed when they can neither see nor smell. These three main senses determine the methods used by pike anglers. Thus we use deadbaits to exploit the pike's ability to smell out and scavenge; the livebait to exploit sight (and the fact that live fish are the pike's prime food source); and the artificial lure to exploit all three senses, but perhaps particularly that of vibration detection. Learn to exploit all three senses yourself, and understand the breadth of techniques, you will be very successful. If you restrict yourself to one technique your results will be poor. Be versatile and open minded.

Sight Perhaps the easiest way for a pike angler to judge the distance a pike can see is to note the distance from which it takes off when it targets a lure. Obviously, this can only be done in shallow water because you need to see the take-off boil, as well as being able to measure that point to the position of the lure at the time. I have done this on several occasions now and there is no doubt in my mind that pike can see a lure from at least 25yd away. In reality, in clear water, it can probably see much further, but the distance may be too great for it to think about the lure as an attractive food item. What this means for the pike angler is that in clear water the splash of the bait entering the water might well be seen by pike in excess of a 50yd circle centred on the bait. In coloured water it may be less.

   On many occasions the pike may miss the lure despite what seemed like a furious and definite attack. There are several possible explanations for this, but the one I like best is that a split second before the pike hits the lure it has to open its mouth. As it does so the upper jaw is raised and this automatically cuts out the pike's vision. If the lure is being retrieved erratically or quickly, the pike might easily miss at that precise moment. Of course, when the pike's mouth opens, it goes into automatic pilot, using sensory canals in its head to detect the position of the prey by its vibrations. This might be less efficent than sight itself.

   The pike's eyes are located on the top of its head, more or less, and it has good sideways, forward and upwards vision. Often it targets a prey from below, coming quickly out of the murk at the strike, but it may have crept upwards for some distance before attacking. Echo-sounders show that a pike about to attack will orientate itself more or less vertically and creep upwards on the ready. But in the many shallow waters pike cannot do this; it is quickly obvious that their forward and sideways vision is good too.

Vibrations It can easily be demonstrated that the pike vibration detection system is important and functions well. Pike that are totally blind or blind in one eye will fall to the lure rod, and spinning in coloured water is possibly less productive than spinning in the dark and the pike may have more difficulties here. This does suggest that even in the dark the pike's eyes function to a degree and it is able to target a black silhouette – either that, or the turbulence normally associated with coloured water in a river actually complicates the vibration patterns received by the pike.

   The vibration detection system used by pike is common among fish. It consists of a canal system linked by pores to the surface of the body. Look at the pike's head, or along its lateral line, you will see a series of obvious pores.

The sleek form of an autumn pike being returned to the water

These connect to a tube or canal system just below the surface of the skin; any change in 'pressure', such as that caused by the nearness of an object to the fish's body, results in compression of the fluid in the canal and this message is transmitted very accurately to the brain and the shape of the object is identified. It is not unlike our radar detection systems. Coupled with direct and good vision, this detection system makes the pike an efficient predator.

Apart from the fact that sight may be shut off at the moment of impact, another variable the pike angler has to weigh up is that the very flash of his lures, which are used initially to attract the pike's interest, may actually confuse the pike's vision as it homes in for the kill. The pike on the attack is like a targeting missile using all its systems. However, the pike is a short-haul missile. It does not track its target at speeds like the perch, worrying it and damaging it until it slows down. The pike 'calculates' the distance and speed it needs, works out whether the effort is worthwhile, and then fires itself. Its object is to engulf its prey in its maw. All lure fishermen will experience this often, even lures as large as 10in will completely disappear into the mouth of a 20lb pike.

Smell Most British anglers recognise this facility that the pike has and they pander to it by adding smells to the bait, the groundbait or to the water itself. Nowadays it is possible to buy pilchard oil (originally introduced for sea fishing), mackerel oil, smelt oil, etc, which can be utilised in various ways (see Chapter 3). At this stage I simply wish to make the point that the pike seems to home in well on a deadbait laid upon the bottom of the water. It may not see it arrive and it certainly does not feel its vibrations. But it sniffs it out. Very little observation has been carried out on the way in which a pike picks up a deadbait, which is important with regard to the hooking and striking out system in use at the time. They certainly pick them up crossways in their jaws as a rule, just as they hit a livebait or live fish and hold it in the same way. Whenever I have watched a pike turn a herring I cannot say that I could see clearly what happened. One second the bait was crossways, with the head and tail sticking out on either side, and the next I could see only the tail sticking out of the front. I saw no jaw movement, no opening and shutting of the mouth. In fact, I concluded that the tongue, which is armed with a veritable file of tiny teeth, had done the turning, the jaws perhaps opening to a minimum – as would be preferable if the pike had a still lively fish across its jaws. Perhaps those who have observed this regularly, or perhaps fed them in tanks, could enlighten us on this score. If the pike does turn the bait with little further opening of its jaws, then there are two implications for the size and position of the hooks: too large and they will get in the way, making timing of the strike more difficult; placed incorrectly and they will not secure a purchase at all.

Speed and Acceleration Some seasons ago I crudely estimated, that on a water where I could see everything, the big pike were covering 20yd and more in not much over one second – that is, they travelled at least twenty times their own body length in one second, which is considerably greater than some claimed scientific figures of 5–7 body lengths per second (about 8mph). My own observations on tiny pike fry is that they can cover about 9yd in one second – about thirty times their own body length in one second. The actual figures do not matter much, of course. It is enough to appreciate that pike can overhaul by this astonishing acceleration almost all freshwater fish, as long as they do not have to maintain the speed. I do not think that trout have quite the same acceleration, but I suspect they could be outpacing a pike by the time forty yards was up: before that they probably rely on their unrivalled agility.

The acceleration from a standing start is no doubt achieved by the grouping at the rear of the fish of the dorsal, anal and caudal (tail) fins, the pectoral and pelvic fins (which are much smaller) merely acting as brakes, stabilisers and anti-roll devices. Thus a mighty thrust of the back end of the fish drives it forward, and its pointed anterior end and wedge-shaped snout cut through the water like a rocket. The main part of the body itself can be seen to work with a rapid sinuous movement, muscle packs on the flanks of the fish being brought alternatively into play. All this is done at great speed and clearly anti-roll mechanisms, and brakes, must operate. Another feature of a rapid pike attack is that it can stop dead in its tracks

PIKE ECOLOGY

Let us turn now to the role of pike in the ecology of a water. If it has all the above weapons going for it, why should any prey survive at all? The fact is that pike have been on Earth for about eighty million years and they haven't succeeded in eating themselves out of house and home! That, of course, is the point not appreciated by those humans who are anti-pike: the pike lives in a state of shifting balance with its prey supply. If the prey declines in numbers then the pike has to follow suit.

That said, the best growth rates for pike will be in waters where there is a good food supply, especially if there is a bonus supply of some kind. Size of water is important: very small waters of, say 5 acres, can produce 30lb pike if there is a superabundance of food. But in all probability they will yield only one such fish at any one time. Big waters with the same facility will produce numbers of giants, especially if the big ones have a chance of culling out their own species before *they* get too big and themselves indent the food supply.

Weight of Food Eaten It seems likely that a big pike can maintain its weight, but not grow, if it eats its own body weight in a year. So a 20lb pike could maintain that size by eating 20lb of fish in a year, which averages at about $1/2$oz of food per day. This probably explains the pike's widespread distribution as one of the main circumpolar predators in the freshwater of the northern hemisphere: it can obviously exist until food supplies increase.

To ensure a steady growth rate it seems that a pike needs to eat between 4 $\times$ and 7 $\times$ per pound of its body weight, per annum. Thus a 20lb fish putting on 2lb per year, probably has to eat 80–100lb of prey per annum, which works out at an average of 4oz of food per day.

There is a debate as to how many pike a water can contain in terms of the well-being of the cyprinids – that is, prey species. The generally accepted wisdom of fisheries scientists seems to argue for a biomass ratio of 1:10 as preferable, possibly decreasing to 1:7 in very productive waters – that is, every ton of pike needs 7 tons of food fish. Looked at very roughly, this means that 2,240lb of pike could be supported by 15,680lb of cyprinids. If the pike were all ten-pounders, then to grow 2lb of body weight they would eat 224 $\times$ 2 $\times$ 365lb per annum, 10,200lb, or rather less than 4 tons of the 7 tons. But 224 $\times$ 10lb fish are an impossibility in our sample ton; more likely would be about 20 $\times$ 10lb fish, plus a few large fish and lots of smaller ones. The 10lb fish would only eat 912lb to grow to a 12lb fish in one year. All this ignores the cyprinid productivity, which may be very high, and the tendency of pike to eat pike – that is, *ie*, recycled cyprinids. In actual fact, a healthily growing population comprising 1 ton of pike probably eats 2 tons of cyprinids, or less.

My own feeling, based upon experience of some very productive fisheries, is that this ratio guide of 1:7 is wrong. I am certain that in good waters 1 ton of pike will be supported by as little as 3 tons of cyprinids. In short, those anglers who fish for other species have nothing to fear from the pike.

The food conversion figures given above also explain why the winter pike fisherman has a struggle to catch in very cold weather. One suspects that when it is close to freezing, a large number of pike do not feed at all, let alone sample 4oz of food. Their metabolism slows down as drastically as that of the pike angler sitting on the bank.

The actual growth rate of pike is not an easy matter to determine. In the first ten years of life the pike's scales can be read successfully. After that they are difficult to read, and it may be that once the maximum length is almost achieved, additions to the skeletal components stop. This does not mean to say that the fish do not put on weight, of course. The slightest increase in body length might result in many pounds being added to the weight. It does seem that an average of 3lb growth in a year is good going for any pike. Many pike grow at a rate of only 2lb a year and only in the most unusual waters is the rate as high as 5lb a year.

Shoulder scale from a fish about 12 to 13 years old, with well-marked annular rings. This was a 20lb fish, 38½ inches long by 20 inches girth

Prey Species The greatest culler of small pike is large pike, which selectively prey on small pike if the numbers of the latter increase too much. It does follow from this that it is a serious error of judgement to remove large pike from any water, unless you wish to encourage an upsurge in the number of small pike. Only one thing keeps down the number of small pike, and that is large pike.

Some years ago I studied the pike removal figures from thirty Irish trout waters over a ten-year period. The pike removal figures were published annually by the Inland Fisheries Trust, and, no doubt, the Irish trout anglers loved to see them. I cannot think why. Had they studied them closely they would have observed the following:

1 After an initial decline in pike tonnage, which is usually seen only in the first year or two years, the tonnage of pike increased.

2 The average size of pike decreased, so that the increased tonnage was a result of more pike, but of smaller size. (After a few years the average weight of these pike was $1\frac{1}{2}$lb.)

3 The total cost ran into millions of pounds.

The conclusions are obvious. If you wish to increase predation on your stock fish, be they trout or cyprinids, remove as many large pike as possible.

Should you get an increase in jacks naturally, then the big pike will target them. This is known as the *buffer effect*. It works in other situations, too. For example, Lake Windermere once had a huge perch population which the pike selectively preyed upon. When all the perch died from disease, the pike turned to the next available food source in good supply – game fish. Again, the message is clear. If you wish to distract the pike from your preferred sport fish, you must put in a buffer species between the pike and your preferred species. In a trout reservoir it pays to leave in the cyprinids and pike; reduce the number of cyprinids and pike by netting, the remaining (more numerous) jacks will turn on the trout. Equally, if you have quality roach fishing that you wish to artificially protect from pike, then my advice is to feed the pike quantities of offal or dead fish. This will benefit the pike angler and the roach.

Pike have lived in harmony with their environment over the centuries until man began to persecute them as vermin, with the result that quality pike fisheries have been all but destroyed. Nothing else has ever benefited from this approach either. Things are beginning to change, and only the modern trout manager is now out of step with the times as he seeks to remove both buffer species and their predator. Big trout waters cannot be run like small trout streams, where all competitors to the trout can usually be eradicated for a while.

BAROMETRIC PRESSURE

The influence of barometric pressure on the feeding behaviour of pike is a controversial issue. In any pressure system the weather, although broadly the same, actually varies considerably on any one occasion. Recently I plotted the conditions of wind, sun, rain etc on a single high-pressure cell hovering over the UK. In different parts of the country it was warm and sunny; cold and with strong winds and rain; snowing; freezing; and the wind directions were locally variable (because they were travelling around a high-pressure cell of some size). The one constant factor over the UK was that the pressure had just risen strongly, was higher by far than the previous week, and was heading for a peak all over. On that particular weekend, with a suddenly rising barometer, the pike came on the feed all over the country. Many big fish were taken. Yet some were taken under still, foggy conditions, some under a bright sun, while others were taken under a gale force wind.

Although it has been known for decades that on a rising barometer trout tend to be active and come on the feed, what is not appreciated is what happens on a *low* barometer. Now, there was a French experiment or observation about fifteen years ago, in which trout in a very large, deep, *indoor* tank were observed. It was noticed repeatedly that when the pressure was high the trout became very active, rose in the water, and tended to feed in the upper layers and on the surface. When the barometer was down, so were the trout, and if they were active at all they grubbed about on the bottom. The importance of this work is that it eliminates wind, rain, and sun and everything by way of weather that one normally sees out of doors! Only B.P. and the moon could exert any influence, the temperature being constant.

As a broad scenario it is the same with pike: under low pressure conditions, they will feed on deadbaits on the bottom, and even have a tendency to do so when they are generally off the feed; on a high barometer they will be more active and more likely to fall to lures and livebaits, except on waters under, say, 8ft deep when they will feed on whatever they can find (because they are actively on the hunt).

It is necessary to watch the barometer from day to day to gauge the pressure accurately. For the last three years, I have had access to a continuous graph print-out and I mark it up with all the catches that my friends and I make. As I can plot them on the chart very exactly, the graph makes interesting study after a few months. The importance of regularly watching pressure is this. Suppose the barometric pressure has been low for some time, say a week, and then it rises steeply over a twelve-hour period. The greater feeding activity of the hunting type occurs *as the barometer starts to rise*, and may well be over after much less than twelve hours, even if the barometer continues to rise for another week. Nevertheless, fish that are caught will usually be to active

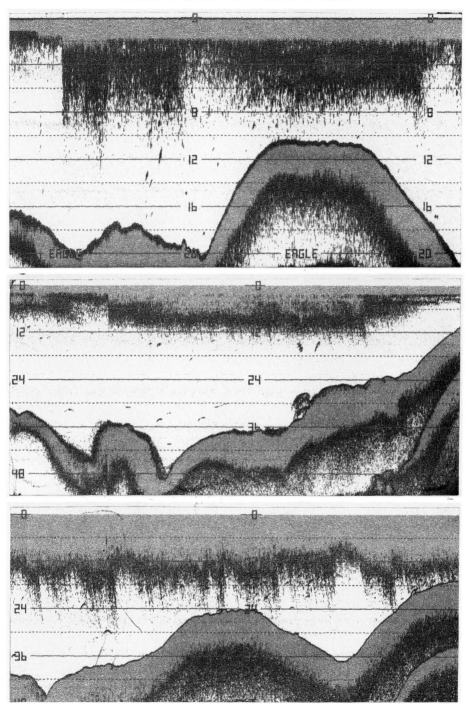

Barometric pressure graph recordings

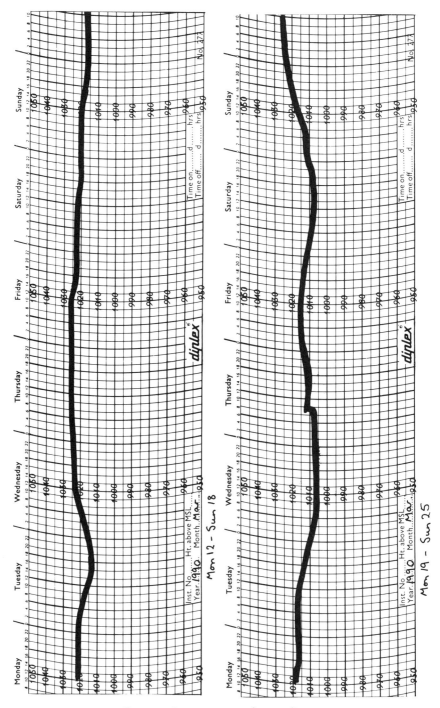

Barometric pressure graph recordings

methods unless the water is shallow.

Those occasions when hunting pike are everywhere, seemingly, and feeding madly, are on just those occasions when the barometric pressure has risen sharply after a long, low spell. It is on these occasions that the big pike move out of the hotspots and hunt far and wide. The feeding urges can go in phases, but often it is the different sized groupings that are feeding. Thus the little ones wait until the big ones have finished. The end of a big fish feeding spree is often characterised by a number of smaller fish falling to the angler – like the lesser catches made the day after a really big catch.

My experience is that whenever the pressure goes down sharply the pike go off the feed. The longer the pressure is down, the more likely the pike are to feed on deadbaits on the bottom. I have known periods when pike have fed exclusively on deadbaits for three weeks at a time, totally ignoring livebaits, apart from the odd jack pike. Sometimes, in a very 'settled' spell of low pressure you can catch plenty of good fish on deadbaits, although this does seem to depend on the water. However, some pike dislike scavenging on the bottom, and probably just sit there doing nothing.

One angler in Kent maintains that the actual reading in millibars is important, and that pike feed in particular ways in particular bands, but my own observations are not that sophisiticated. However, I am now sure that when big pike are feeling sluggish and on the bottom in a low pressure system, the smaller pike can be active and caught on lures. It does not need a great stretch of the imagination to see why.

I am still uncertain as to whether the moon phase is important. It certainly is in any tidal fishing, including the sea, and many anglers in the USA swear by it. Intuitively one feels that some combinations of pressure and moon phase ought to affect the activities of pike if pressure alone certainly does, but I have not done sufficient work on the subject to reach any conclusions.

Among those anglers who do believe in and operate on the influence of barometric pressure, no one has come up with a *reason* for its effect. Possibly, under low pressure systems there is a tendency for water to evaporate at the air/water interface and for O_2 to be lost from the water. If the temperature starts to drop at the surface, and the water simultaneously starts to deoxygenate, this could explain why the pike loses it *joie de vivre*.

2

EQUIPMENT AND TACKLE

All anglers accumulate mountains of equipment, and I am no exception. When setting off on a pike trip my vehicle is loaded, seemingly, as though I'm off for a month. In this chapter I want to describe all my kit, why I want it and how I use it.

The first thing I would consider is something to carry all the junk in.

Rucksack Your choice of rucksack is very important, but it cannot be too large for bait-fishing trips. At present I use a 110 litre SAS rucksack, A-frame rather than the modern H-frame, for carrying all my equipment. Its only real drawback is that with its steel frame it takes an average SAS man to carry it; but I understand that the latest versions have a carbon-fibre frame. I have tried, in the past, various boxes and baskets, but they are very inefficient. If you have to walk any distance, they cannot be shouldered without pain and a trolley is impracticable. I do have a trolley for certain long, easy – that is, level – walks, when they are invaluable. I use an A-frame rucksack because it doesn't fall over when it is placed on the ground. Also, when weight is at a premium and one's chair has been dispensed with, one can sit on a polythene sheet on the grass and lean against the rucksack as a comfortable backrest. Unfortunately, A-frame rucksacks are now a rarity.

Nowadays, specialist angling luggage is increasingly available and the new ruckbags are excellent. Several firms make them, and in essence they are like a holdall bag that you can strap up to carry like a rucksack. Some specialist angling luggage, which has only recently been introduced, is the Wychwood range, and it has some superb rucksacks in its collection. I am also very impressed with the giant Shakespeare bag, which was produced in 1991. I may well replace my SAS rucksack with this bag as it is strong, light and of a good countryside colour, although I will lose the backrest facility of the A-frame.

Rod Holdall In the past these were ill-designed on the golf-bag principle, into which you pushed your rods etc with difficulty, often denuding them of rod rings in the process. So I and colleagues 'invented' a roll-up holdall that took about five rods, made up (minus only the reel body), umbrella and rod rests,

Even big, wide, fenland drains can have their attractions; this is the Relief Cut-off Channel near Denver, Norfolk

Barrie Rickards' winter camp for a session of static deadbait fishing

plus a landing-net handle. Those were, and are, very compact and efficient and they were eventually manufactured on a huge scale.

However, some better custom-built holdalls are available now, and the one I use mostly was made by E.T. Tackle. This takes four rods, made up, complete with reels, plus all the other items listed in the previous paragraph. My objective is to get everything I need into one of these holdalls and my rucksack. This leaves me *two* hands free, one of which may be needed to carry a bait bucket, and I am always able to open gates, climb stiles, and tuck my hands into the rucksack straps to ease the weight, shift the position, and so on. Relatively recently, some rod slings have come onto the market. These are similar to quivers, and are very light. The rods, with reels and tackle attached, can be stuck in them either in the doubled-up position or fully assembled ready for action.

Bait Buckets These are now designed to suit the angler. I have two that are excellent, a big black one designed by E.T. Tackle, and a smaller fold-away one made by Shakespeare. The ingenious Shakespeare bucket I use for short trips and a small number of baits; otherwise I carry it in the rucksack, folded away, in case I get any baits during fishing. The larger box has an internal plastic cage that enables you to lift out a few fish without getting your hands frozen; it also enables you to sink the bait in the water for maximum oxygenation. It is based on the ancient zinc bait bucket idea but is brilliantly executed for the modern angler. For the aerator there is only one choice – Shakespeare do the ultimate convenient aerator and rightly lead the field. I once did a battery check, and although you pay twice the price, at least, for Duracell batteries, you get up to five times the life out of them. I can see no improvement in the E.T. bait bucket or the Shakespeare aerator. Both are perfectly suited to the modern piker, however much of a specialist he considers himself.

Chair For many years I have used lightweight garden chairs, which are suitable, if not bulky and a little upright. The colours tend to be garish; they cannot be adjusted for difficult banks, and they are not comfortable enough to lounge in for more than an hour or so. I recently bought myself a Fox International Multi-adjustable chair from Trevor Moss in Gainsborough. They have no arms and are very expensive, but they are simply the best chairs I have ever come across. All four legs are adjustable and the chair can be set out quite low to the horizon, or up high, and can also be operated on steeply sloping banks. They are, however, rather heavy, as befits their robust construction.

I will not go into the question of brolly camps/bivvies and camping equipment, because those items are the same for all types of fishing. Suffice it to say that I use them often, and night fishing should not be dismissed for piking – it can be a fast and furious sport.

A number of other items stay in my car while I am fishing. I have a sack with spare clothes in case I fall in, including an extra one-piece suit of old design. I also carry spare thermal boots. In tackle terms I have a plastic lure box full of lures; you cannot wander the bank carrying this, but at least you can increase your choice for the day by having them available. There is also a spare cooker as well as additional food in the form of Hotcans, and fluid. The last is very important in summer when lack of planning can lead to dehydration. Almost equally often there is a pile of boat fishing equipment, but discussion of that I shall leave until Chapter 6. Finally, I carry some weed-cutting tools, a drag and a cutter. It is surprising how often you need a cutter – for example, when you are starting on a brand new water (see Chapter 6).

Tackle in the Rucksack and Holdall Almost always I carry a small lightweight pair of binoculars for observing wildlife and for keeping my eyes on rising fish. On a new water it is sometimes useful to scan distant swims, so they do have a general usefulness. I would not be without them unless I had a very long way to walk. My camera is a Canon AE1, which has a good lens and I carry a telephoto lens too. However, it is undeniably heavy, so unless I have a special assignment, I tend to carry only a small compact camera – a Pentax with a zoom lens which fits easily into the bottom of one of the side pockets of the rucksack.

In the bottom of the rucksack I carry a few spare items that might be of value: large polythene bags (useful for putting over your feet if your get them wet and have to put on wet socks again, or for mixing up bait in); a coil of string (nylon); spare mittens and a balaclava (you can be miles from anywhere when the bad weather sets in) and usually a spare reel. I always carry a couple of spare spools with pike line on them, just in case I lose some line or it goes 'off', but these are in the bottom of one of the rucksack's side pockets along with a Swiss Army knife and a small torch (a large torch is always in the car).

On my giant rucksack the two very large side pockets were stitched down their long sides only, not across the bottom. I stitched this up so that I have two very slim, extra pockets, into which I fit a knife for dealing with deadbaits (a Shakespeare filleting knife), a dial balance (Kevin Nash type), and my forceps. A much more powerful spring balance, a Salter going up to 50lb, is wrapped in an oiled rag in the car.

I also carry a keepsack which I rarely use, and this is folded small and pushed into one of the side pockets as packing as much as anything else. Like my weighing sling, it is E.T. Tackle in origin and well designed for the job. The weighing sling is very smooth and when wet it weighs 10oz; of course, the dial balance is adjusted to zero, but if I have to use it on an ordinary spring balance I know how much to knock off.

In the days when I carried a large but upright chair I also had a piece of rather bulky foam rubber to put on it; but the Fox International has its own tastefully padded seat in dark camouflaged green. So that saves some space and my flask and food now fit tightly and my sandwiches get less squashed.

For winter fishing you need to be warm and comfortable, and cooking a hot meal on the bankside will help you to achieve this state. I usually carry two cookers, a small petrol stove which stays in the car (but which fits very comfortably in a side pocket of the rucksack for when it is needed), and a Gaz cooker which has a small stand for uneven banks. This and the associated gear, such as pan, grub and water, are carried in a green canvas bag which I then squeeze into the top of the rucksack after the frozen deadbaits have gone in. A folding aluminium windshield, which is compact and light, is a useful addition for the outdoor cook. There is nothing like a cup of tea or coffee brewed fresh, and, coupled with bacon, eggs and sausages on a cold winter's day, it becomes a great way to wait for the big pike to bite.

Clothes Do invest in thermal underwear, otherwise your comfort may decline to a degree that makes fishing dangerous. If you wear one of the one-piece waterproof, windproof outfits, the worst you will suffer from is being too warm. When a long walk down the river bank is in the offing, take off the suit, roll it up and tie it to the rucksack. After cooling down on arrival, you can put the suit back on and stay warm. If you go without warm clothing you could get caught out in bad conditions and suffer from hypothermia, with serious consequences.

One-man boat system. Subsequent to this overhaul the gunwales were fitted with pipe lagging so that rods could be dropped on them without damage

As a two-man craft it is more doubtful! Note the pipe lagging on the gunwales

'Groundbaiting' is best done in a basket of wire. Cormorants cannot eat the bait! The attractant must be replaced once a week, otherwise it is capable of walking to the bank!

Garish orange or red lures, whether plug or spoon, are a must in any lure bag, for on occasions they out-scare all others

A deadly set of lures: K12 Kwikfish jointed plug in coachdog finish; Barrie's Buzzer; and some Kilty and Landa lures in good pikey colours

Waders are cumbersome to walk in but nowadays the thermal waders are so good that I wouldn't be without them. Thermal boots are fine, but they don't keep your thighs warm on really cold days. A useful tip for keeping your waders pulled up is to wear a pair of braces and attach them to those. If you attach them to the waistband of your trousers you will pull your trousers down. Hats are a person choice, but I have a variety, some waterproof ones as well as other types.

Gloves are not so much an item to keep the hands warm, but rather something with which to handle pike carefully. I have two pairs which adequately serve both purposes. The first pair are light yellow, soft leather, gardening gloves, with elasticated wrists. These are excellent as an unhooking aid because they both protect the fingers and at the same time are soft and gentle on the pike. The second pair will serve the same purpose, but cost about £4 rather than £11, are soft, black plastic (pseudo-leather) and have long elasticated wrists. However, these can be worn for spinning in cold weather which the real leather ones cannot. The disadvantage of the plastic gloves is that they are not as waterproof and as warm as the leather ones.

There are some new gloves on the market which derive, I believe, from scuba divers' kit. Shakespeare produces them with and without fingers, but I would never opt for fingerless gloves – all that happens is that your fingers get very cold. The full gloves are very warm.

Your choice of clothing between your thermals and your suit, is a matter of personal preference. There is ample room for a jacket underneath your suit, although I usually wear just one or two sweaters and a woollen shirt, and, of course, trousers. If there is one area where one-piece suits need improving it is in the provision of pockets. I have a Belstaff which has a tendency to come apart at the seams, but is not as stiff as some suits. Its pockets are warm but far too small and too few. My stiffer, more robust suit is called a Mainstream. This has a quilted lining and is wind- and waterproof; perhaps its only drawback – apart from inadequate cold pockets – is that the front, when zipped up, digs into the neck and chin; that area could certainly be improved. A scarf around the neck helps to keep you warm, but better than that is what the army call a headover. This is a tube of warm woollen material that you pull over your head. It can be worn as a 'scarf' or as a woollen hat. I cadged mine off that fanatical lure fisherman Fred Blandford when he was based at Waterbeach Barracks. Unlike scarves, these headovers don't come adrift. On the other hand, you can't tie up bundles of rods with them as I recently did with a scarf, for Colin Dyson!

The same clothes are needed for winter lure fishing as for bait fishing. It is a fallacy that lure fishing in winter keeps you warm. It does not. When lure fishing, you work the bank *slowly*, and you are fully exposed to the elements, so you need all the protection of the bait fisherman, except that you do not have

The author about to return a good reservoir pike. Note the gloved left hand, and correct holding of the fish.

his umbrella. I tend to lure fish in the depths of winter as an adjunct to bait fishing so that I have a base camp and warm food to go to. I do not usually lure fish in cold weather for more than half an hour, after which I need to desist for a while to warm up. The results may be worthwhile, so never dismiss cold weather spinning as a waste of time.

Clothing is much easier for the lure angler to organise when fishing in the summer or autumn. Often it is possible to wear only a light shirt. It is most important to keep a sweater and a waterproof in reserve, in your backpack. I have been caught in very wintry weather some 6 miles away from the car, and it can be no joke. A sweater can, of course, be tied around your waist out of the way.

Backpack A small rucksack is essential. I have designed a specialist lure fisherman's bag, but commercial firms are not interested in producing it.

The backpack bag is designed to carry your day's needs without your stack of lures getting into an unhealthy tangle, and also so that the things you need are accessible and in the order in which you need them. As you unzip the lid the first thing you see is the lure roll. This is because you'll be using the bag for lure changes more often than anything else. Simply unroll the lure roll part, select a lure, replace the old one, and roll it up again. You will have no tangling, and it will hold upwards of thirty plugs, spoons and spinners. In addition, the bag hold a small camera, waterproof, balance, forceps, food and drink.

Other lure carriers are no help if you intend to walk the bank. The plastic expandable tool-box style lure holders are excellent for boat anglers or for storing a mass of lures in the car; I use the giant Shakespeare box regularly, which is the best in the UK. But they cannot be lugged along the bank. Even more useless are the small boxes that hold half-a-dozen lures. No serious lure angler should set off with a mere handful of lures. Hook guards are fine, but you need hundreds, and they do not fit all hooks. Furthermore, they can be dangerous when they jam on a treble. If you cannot make a lure bag to my design, or a similar one, it would be better to carry your lures in a lightweight plastic bucket. Everything will get tangled up, but at least the hooks are safe and you can more or less see what you want.

Landing Net Micromesh is disastrous for the lure angler (and in my view, for any pike angler) because hooks get very badly tangled in them, and they can be a danger to pike. The delay factor in unhooking is one reason but also the pike may roll on the snagged hooks and damage itself unnecessarily. I use a 1in mesh of knitted material, which I obtain from Cabela's in Nebraska, which gives no problems at all and I say that without any hesitation or exaggeration. All my angling colleagues will confirm it. I have seen an angler take nearly half an hour to get his hooks out of micromesh, and ten-minute delays are far

The author making a departure from his usual practice by using a huge triangular landing net instead of his preferred round net frame. The result is the same, namely a fine pike

from uncommon. On the other hand, a ten-second delay is the longest I have to tolerate.

Net Frame I am aware that many anglers prefer, inexplicably, those modern triangular nets. They may be suitable for carp fishing, but I doubt their value for pike on many grounds. However, for lure anglers they are useless, because they become tangled in vegetation whenever one moves along the bank. When fishing overgrown banks they are impossible to use. A round frame with a diameter of 30in is quite adequate, and it can be pulled through bushes by holding the rim and pulling it so that the handle follows behind. There are no corners to get caught up and the overall effective diameter of a net of this size is as good as a 40in armed frame of the triangular kind.

Finally, it should not be forgotten that all piking is not done in stillwaters. In river piking, of which there are many exponents (see Sidley, 1987) a micromesh net can bulge in the current and this can be dangerous to the wading angler, as well as inefficient from the netting point of view. And the points of a triangular net are an added danger area.

Rods Carbon has transformed things for the lure fisherman and one can fish all day with rods from 4 to 12ft long, without a rest. I would not recommend fishing in that manner, but it helps to make the point that carbon rods are light. The only warning I would make to a wandering lure fisherman and his

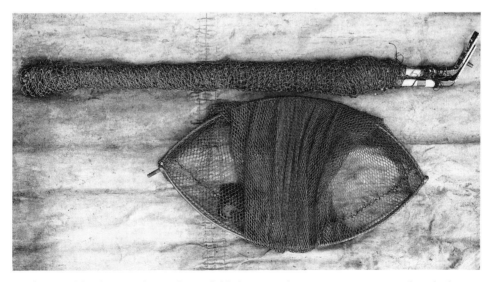

The round landing-net frame shown folded into its three sections, as opposed to the long arms of the triangular net (above). The latter goes into the holdall more easily, but pike go into the former much more readily!

A robust and cheap landing net frame can easily be made from a cycle wheel rim. Note also the wide mesh of the net, a great advantage in piking

carbon rods is that he should watch out for power lines. Remember, you may be wandering the banks for miles, unlike the bottom or pike bait fisherman, and it is quite easy to walk into dangerous territory quite unthinkingly and I've done it myself. If your water does have power lines either crossing it or alongside it, then it is advisable to use a glass rod only.

I use all lengths of rods from 4 to 12ft, as either the inclination or the need commands. There are, however, some generalisations. For boat fishing I would avoid the longer rods and keep to 4–9ft lengths. From banksides where extensive weed, rush or reed growth occurs, avoid the short rods. On the other hand, short rods have their value on banks that are densely overgrown with trees; if you are crawling along on your hands and knees beneath willows, you will find a 4–5ft rod far more comfortable. Alternatively, you can use a telescopic rod.

Rods for lure fishing need to be less powerful than those for bait fishing, but should be slightly stiffer, with more of a tip action. In terms of test curve you need about $1^{1}/_{3}$–2lb. With very short rods the actual test curve becomes meaningless with a rod as powerful as a pike rod, hence one judges by action and feel. The stiff action is to set the hooks and to fire the lure sharply and accurately on the cast. It is important to realise that when you are using spoons and spinners the hooks will usually fetch up against the hard, bony mouth of the pike, allowing little room for soft tissue grip – hence a slightly stiffer action is needed. With short rods this is doubly important because the stiffness helps accuracy. Longer lure fishing rods could be softer from the casting point of view, but you still need steeliness to set the hooks. It is therefore best to avoid through action rods for lure fishing.

The rods I use include the Ryobi spinning rod, either with a crank handle for multiplier use, or the straight handle for fixed spool use. Another excellent rod of moderate length is the Shakespeare Purist Spin, which gives top-class action for pike. In the very short rods I use a one-piece Eaglehawk, of various weights (with multipliers) and the Beulite (so-called) worm (for multipliers, made by Shakespeare).

For bait fishing a huge range of rods, mostly to good design, is available from a number of manufacturers. It is important to have a test curve of about 2–$2^{1}/_{2}$lb (perhaps $2^{1}/_{2}$lb for heavy work), and a length of 10–13ft. I make the length judgement on modern material capabilities, and I would go for 12ft as my preferred length at present. The action of such rods should be through action – that is, a progressive or 'soft' action – for casting baits like half a mackerel, whole herring, and so on, and a fast or tip action for throwing heavy leads coupled with smaller baits. As it happens, I would have made these statements in the days of glass rods, when such considerations were crucial, but with carbon rods matters are less crucial and the material is not only lightweight, but very forgiving.

Cosmetics on these rods are not as important as the length and action and test curve. However, I do have some personal preferences which I shall give to you to take on board or reject as you see fit. First, the weather is often cold for piking and cork seems warmer to the touch than some other materials. Duplon I do not mind, but in wet weather it soaks up water. Artificial cork is also suitable but not as aesthetically appealing as cork itself. It is a question of personal preference, but in bitterly cold weather I find that cork is appreciated. The handles I prefer to be one-piece – rather than separate grips – parallel sided, and with neat shoulders at the top and bottom. The lengths of rod handles tend to be rather long, up to 30in, when they were introduced in the 1950s, the idea was to enable anglers to spread their hands apart for distance casting with the reel at the top of the handle (for the first time in history of the sport). This was probably good design for the very progressive and soft action of rods like the split cane MkIV and MkIV Avon, but with modern rods a handle length of 24in maximum is all that is necessary. Carbon rods, and even slow action rods or those with a wide diameter (thin-walled) butt piece, do cut through the air quickly, so a widespread grip is not necessary any longer for power. For lure fishing a handle of 20in is better because frequently the rod butt will need to be passed across the front of the body.

The modern Fuji reel fittings tended to replace the old sliding winch fittings completely in the 1980s, and this is no bad thing, for they are light and the reel cannot fall off. This was always more likely to happen with big fish when sliding winch fittings were in use, because big fish were more likely to bend that part of the butt piece *within the handle*; when the reel seating of a fixed spool reel is *beneath* the handle, it is just that part which is concave on bending – hence the grip is opened and the reel drops off.

Reels In general, modern reels are superior to all except the most expensive of the older models. The carbon composition of some reels does make them almost unbreakable, and the smoothness of retrieve is something which lasts a long time. All the manufacturers produce reels suitable for piking, at least as far as fixed spool reels are concerned. As long as they have a capacity for 150yd of 15lb breaking strain line they will be good for most pike angling. With that capacity, the reel itself will tend to be of a certain size – about the size of a Mitchell 300, although different models will have a larger casing, skirted spool, circular rear drag button, and so on. As a rough guidance for newcomers, if the reel looks more like a sea reel, then it is too big; if it is match size, it is too small. This is a generalisation: the first is a case of aesthetics rather than practicality, and the second is not strictly true, for the match-sized reels are good for the angler who prefers to travel lightly.

I do have some reservations about modern fixed spool reels. One is that the spindle connecting the base of the reel handle, through the casing and across the gear assembly, to the position for the opposite handle position (most reels are now ambidextrous), is *weak* and the gear connection sloppy. When striking into a very solid fish this spindle can bend, and on occasion may stay bent. In this case the reel locks solid. In cheaper reels (which currently means most models), this is a real weakness.

Clutch systems today are very reliable, but as I never use mine this refinement is lost on me. I keep mine screwed up tight and give line by letting the fish pull the reel handles backwards, which, with the modern smooth-running reel, is a technique which works even better than in the past. As this happens I trail a fingertip on the flyer, thus effecting a sensitive and minutely adjustable brake.

For some reason multiplier reels frighten off many anglers. Price could be the factor. Actual casting can be an art acquired in about half an hour or so – at least as far as avoiding overruns is concerned. For any given fishing situation in piking, an appropriate multiplier will give you less distance but more accuracy and control. I know some anglers, who I greatly respect, who swear by them for boat fishing; one advantage is that the reel can be knocked out of gear and a run is signified by a beautiful 'tick-tick' sound as line is taken. Of course, the recent introduction of the bait-runner reel gives this facility to the fixed-spool reel fan, although the reel casts are comparable.

I have one major reservation about the choice of multiplier available, and it is this: fixed-spool reels are either ambidextrous or you can get left-hand wind models (for right-handed anglers); relatively few multipliers are ambidextrous and very few offer the necessary left-hand wind facility. Manufacturers of fixed-spool reels make most of their reels for right-handed anglers, quite reasonably as most anglers *are* right handed (that is, they use their strongest hand and arm for holding the rod and playing the fish); most of the multipliers are made for left-handed anglers. The manufacturers are very slow to get the fundamentals correct. I recall that at one time they, and match anglers, argued stongly and wrongly against left-hand wind fixed-spool reels. Now they all use them, thanks to the long battle that Richard Walker fought to get the angling world to see common sense. Nowadays you will hear manufacturers, and some anglers brought up to fish a multiplier cack-handed, argue strongly and wrongly against the left-hand wind multipliers. If you want to get this right, take your trade to those who cater for right-handed anglers, such as Ryobi and Abu (Abu have a nervous history in this respect, but unlike some they are trying).

Specific recommendations are difficult to give, but I like the Ryobi T1 and the (old) Abu 5001C (and its new equivalent). In terms of fixed-spool reels I use ancient Mitchells and, more particularly, modern Shakespeare reels.

Line Nylon monofilament is less of a problem nowadays, although there are certain things to watch. Even the rather brightly coloured lines – blue, for example – are not the shiny lines of the past, and once in the water they don't look too bad. However, they look garish and out of place on the spool and I cannot understand why manufacturers do not produce the vast bulk of line in dull, colourless or in darker colours like grey, brown or black. You can get them in those colours, of course, and those are my preferences simply because they do look less conspicuous in the water as well as on the spool.

It does seem from my own experience that the dark-coloured or brightly coloured lines are more prone to sudden loss of breaking strain. This cannot be due solely to undue stretching – for example, following pulling for a break or snag – because it does not happen with Platil grey lines or with the uncoloured or grey Shakespeare lines, both of which I use all the time. But it does happen with other lines. Manufacturers used to deny that nylon monofil deteriorated under the effect of light, especially strong sunlight, but I cannot now see how they can deny it any longer. Lines which suffer strength loss, *literally overnight*, are those lines which are old, have been on the rod without rewinding and/or which have been snagged. What happens is that the *whole length* of line on the spool goes. I have tested this fact on several occasions. So do not think that you can escape the consequences by stripping off 10yd of line and cutting it adrift.

Apart from the two brands of line I have mentioned there are some others that anglers like, especially Maxima and Sylcast. However, whatever brand

The author with a firm, fat pike which fell to drifted livebait

you choose, do test it each day before fishing. This is not a complicated process: simply take a turn in each hand and see if you can break it easily by pulling the hands apart. If you can, get a new line.

Breaking Strain My preferred range is 12–15lb bs. And with this range (or above), the test I have just mentioned works perfectly: you cannot easily break, by hand-to-hand pulling, lines of this strength, which is about right for most of pike fishing. Occasionally – for example in really snaggy, weedy conditions or when doing a lot of boat fishing – I might go up to 18lb bs. On small streams or when using a tiny lightweight bait-caster rod and little multiplier, I might go down to 6 or 8lb bs. On big, open snag-free waters I prefer 12lb bs because I can distance cast it well, but for most of my fishing where 20lb plus fish are expected, I use 14 or 15lb bs.

Small Item Bag I have a Pearce Lure Bag, which is ideal for keeping tidy, dry *and visible* all those items which you need on a regular basis. Each transparent pocket of which there are twelve, is 7 × 5in and they are held together by an outer case of soft material which fastens together with Velcro. Being flexible rather than rigid, it will push and pull into any available space in the rucksack, without damaging the contents.

The first pair of pockets are those in which I keep my rig-making materials – hooks, swivels, link swivels, trace wire and swivels. I always carry a range of hook sizes, 10–6, and similarly a range of swivel sizes, because if you are using small hooks you do not want to spoil the trace with an over-large swivel.

I have studied trace wires very carefully over a number of years and now normally only carry two types: PDQ (or QED) in 20lb bs and Kevlar and wire (Stahlvorfach JP marketed by Partridge). The Middy wire is also good, so I may also carry a spool or two of that. The Kevlar and wire is relatively new in the UK (1990) and I am still trying it out; however, I am thoroughly satisfied with it, most especially with the fact that you can tie half-blood knots in it.

What one might call trace wire comes in two types: relatively soft but rather thick wire (PDQ), and very fine but stiffer wire. I no longer use the latter, having tried it considerably over a decade. It seems to me that it kinks and twists too easily, Ryder hooks (see pp56–8) cannot be moved along it without twisting it into a spiral, and the wire cannot readily be twisted up by hand when trace making. PDQ has none of these failings, the only 'drawback' being that it is slightly thicker, which I feel is of no importance. The Kevlar and wire may be better than all of them, but we shall have to wait for several full seasons' testing to know for certain.

The hooks I carry are of varied type: singles, Bellars' hooks, barbless, semi-barbless and barbed (especially those with very small barbs). Also in the hook pocket are beads to act against the stop knot of a sliding float rig.

The next two folders contain made-up wire traces which are used for spinning, and also for the upper trace (above the hook trace) which I now *invariably* use in all bait fishing. Many of these are homemade, from the above-mentioned packets, but I also use extensively the Shakespeare spinning traces, and a black plastic-coated trace (the brand name of which is unknown to me). The last is interesting, because I have always been opposed in the past to plastic-coated wire. But these do seem to be hard-wearing and well made. Although I am only able to buy them at intervals in UK shops, I did manage to find a few spools in Australia of the wire itself; this you make up into traces by holding a match or lighter flame beneath two lengths held side by side, so that the plastic anneals one to the other. These are excellent once you have the idea of making them up and, naturally, varied lengths can be made up in no time at all.

The next six or seven pockets have made-up hook traces – snap tackles. At present I either make my own snap tackles or use those by Middy, which are the best commercial ones I have ever used.

The next two pockets contain a mixed bag of items – a container of E.T. Floatant (for drift fishing) which is much better in my view than Mucilin; a few 'dough-bobbin' indicators, consisting of washing-up liquid tops, each fitted with a plastic tube which will take Starlights or Betalights; some Starlights; and also a small emergency kit of Elastoplast and aspirin.

Next, two folders contain giant balloons for drifting, and several types of slim sliding floats (see pp71–2) Another two pockets contain V-shaped, screw-in rod rest tops, 6lb bs paternoster line on a 100m spool, a fistful of rubber bands, an Optonic tightening screw, a tape measure, a compass, spare line clips and an adaptor which connects a camera to a bank-stick. Finally, several pockets house licences and PVA string and tape.

Rod Rests While the rod rest tops are kept in the Pearce Lure Bag, the sticks themselves, six, plus a spare, go into the rod holdall, which was described earlier in this chapter. Three of them may well have the Optonics heads left in position, for the E.T. holdall is nothing if not capacious. The rod rests themselves are telescopic, operated not by means of a screw, but by a neat knurled knob which lies along the axis of the rest, which does not stick out from the side to catch the lines. The top insert is black glass-fibre, and the bottom half, which goes into the ground, is duralumin and also black. With the knob tightened slightly the telescopic effect can be achieved just by pulling – the two parts slide stiffly, which is very convenient on a cold day. Unfortunately, I have been unable to discover who makes them.

SAS rucksack One of the items that goes in the front pocket that needs to be protected is a container with five tubes of 'smells'– that is, smelt oil, mackerel oil, kipper oil, etc. The tubes are not the ones in which you buy them but some chemical bottles which I obtained that have a safety plug beneath the screw cap. Having dispensed a few drops, the top of the bottle can be washed with the safety cap in place, which results in a smell-free rucksack.

I also have a small pouch with varied sizes of lead weights (and substitutes), including 2–3oz leads. Most of these are Arlesey Bombs, but other kinds include Wye leads for lure fishing and anti-kink leads (and casting weight). These can be kept in an old sock, but the small canvas zip-pouch that I use is strong enough to stop the leads knocking other items in the pocket.

A fistful of varied floats, including dull floats for sunken rigs and buoyancy rigs, are kept loose in the pocket. In the end, when they lose too much paint, I replace them and repaint them. A large spool of paternoster line is kept in the same pocket as it is almost constantly in use. The spool in the Pearce Lure Bag is merely a spare or safety spool. At most times of the year I carry a small lure roll, perhaps with half-a-dozen tried and trusted lures and traces, close to hand in the pocket (the telescopic Shakespeare Supra Econ is in the main compartment of the rucksack, complete with reel attached, so that once I have decided to lure fish it can be operational in about thirty seconds).

Another very useful item when bait fishing is the drop-back indicator, a coil of plastic from a bottle of around 1–2in diameter. These can be 1–2in wide, basically white, but coloured Sellotape can be stuck on them to give extra visibility. Having cut a circle from the bottle, one side is slit completely, when the two edges immediately overlap due to the elasticity of the plastic. They can be clipped on and off the line in a few seconds, yet do not blow off with the wind. They can also be weighted with shot or a lead sheet. The actual use of these as a drop-back indicator is explained on p61. I rarely use commercial drop-back indicator/alarms.

The same capacious pocket houses the artery forceps when these are not clipped to my person or to some other conspicuous place; and I usuallly keep a very small torch there for baiting up in near darkness before dawn.

Despite all this equipment there is still sufficient room in the rucksack and/or holdall to take additional items considered necessary on a particular day. One of the hallmarks of inexperienced anglers is that they do not have sufficiently varied equipment, and therefore lack flexibility of approach; another is that their tackle is not well organised. The outfit I have described to you in this chapter not only meets these requirements, but is encompassed only by one rucksack and one holdall (perhaps with a bait bucket). It may be necessarily heavy at times, but equally often it is not. Furthermore, what I have outlined is a complete outfit, excluding boat-fishing equipment. The only 'unsatisfactory' matter at present is the rucksack frame which adds unnecessarily to the weight. However, I shall do something about that before long.

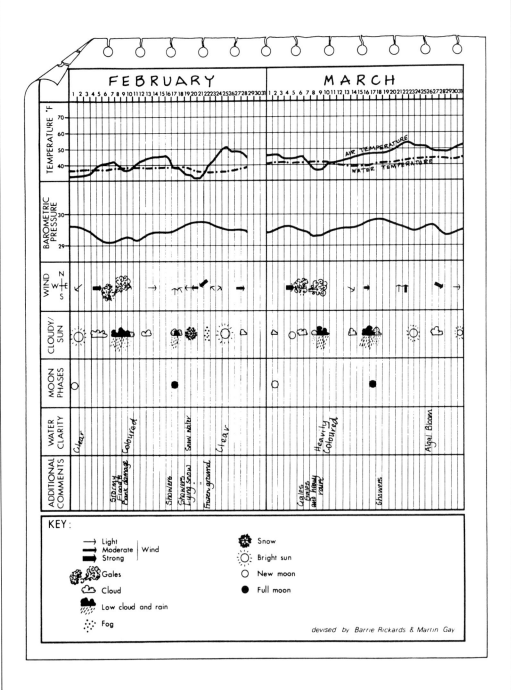

The author's record of angling conditions

EQUIPMENT AND TACKLE

Date: ....   **Venue:** ....

Fishing times: ....

Additional notes on conditions:

Target:

Catch:

THE   DAY / NIGHT

CONCLUSIONS, THOUGHTS etc.

devised by Barrie Rickards & Martin Gay

3

SUCCESSFUL TECHNIQUES

As the pike feeds primarily on live fish, and to a lesser extent on dead and dying fish, the techniques used to effect its capture will involve fish baits, or artificial copies thereof. And they will utilise the three main senses the pike itself uses – namely sight, vibration detection and smell. This rather limits our tactical approaches to the use of live fish (livebaiting), the use of dead fish (deadbaiting – either static or mobile) and the use of imitations of fish (spinners, spoons and plugs). Of the three senses, all are used by the pike when it falls to the live fish; sight and smell are used when it falls to a static dead fish; perhaps all three are used when it falls to a wobbled or spun deadbait; and sight and vibration come into play when a lure succeeds. So, in a sense, there is some flexibility that the pike hunter can employ, but it all hinges on fish, fish and more fish. Attempts to use other baits such as HP boilies or vegetable matter can only be successful infrequently because the pike is not interested as a rule. If such a bait shows movement, then the matter is different; or if a smell of fish is imparted to the boilie – for example, fish meal – then, again, the pike may respond.

It follows from these arguments that a live fish is likely to be the most reliable and consistent bait simply because, at the end of the day, a pike cannot refuse such an offering for ever unless he is spooked and suspicious. In that case, he will actively deselect it in favour of the real thing when he gets really hungry. The live fish *is* the most reliable bait for pike.

Let me nail my own flag to the mast here, clearly and unambiguously, for I have in recent times been misquoted.

My favourite method of pike fishing is the static deadbaiting method. By this means I have just taken one of my best catches, of four pike over 20lb weight in one day. My second favourite method is lure fishing, and in the Introduction I explained how I have taken recently one of the best lure-caught pike catches in history – 850lb in one and a half days. But it is my firm opinion, based upon experience, that neither of these methods is as reliable, consistent or as successful as livebaiting.

I do not subscribe to the view held by some people that livebaiting is cruel. I have argued elsewhere (Rickards, 1986) that there is overwhelming evidence

One of Barrie Rickards' best pike, 31¹/₂lb, to a static ledgered mackerel head

that a fish cannot feel pain from a hook stuck in it, nor does it suffer unduly from being drawn to the bank and netted. It follows from this that it hardly matters *where* the hook is stuck in a fish if it doesn't feel it. I agree that for aesthetic reasons an angler might wish to forgo the use of live fish, and that is a reason I feel is sound. But it is a far cry from arguing cruelty. Indeed, those who do so leave themselves wide open to similar charges relating to the use of *any* livebait, whether worm, maggot or fish. Logic and sound sense wins no arguments here, however, and only prejudice rules.

I tend not to livebait. It is fiddly and time consuming. Deadbaiting and lure fishing are logistically easier and I get my results that way by preference. But I would be more successful – indeed, I was in the past – were I to maintain a *fully* flexible approach and use all the methods available to me. But let us make no fundamental errors of judgement: livebaiting is *the* successful method, followed some way behind by the other methods, and these latter in rather debatable order. In other words, I am unsure which is better, deadbaiting or lure fishing.

DEADBAITING

There have been two misguided attempts to ban deadbaiting on the grounds that it is cruel to pike. One of these was a serious attempt in the late 1950s and it failed because the developing sport rapidly put its house in order. The second was not so much an attempt to ban it as an argument advanced against it in 1989 by Conrad Voss Bark, an experienced game fisherman and journalist. He was badly in error, in my view, in that he seemed to think that today's deadbaiting was carried out as it was in a very short period in the early 1950s. He could not have been more mistaken. These hiccups apart, static deadbaiting is one of the most successful on occasion, and one of the most delightful ways of piking.

The problem hinted at in the previous paragraph concerns the risk that the pike may swallow the bait so deeply that the hooks cannot be removed. This can happen very rarely, but some measure of its rarity can be gauged from the fact that it is well over ten years since it happened to me, and before that I cannot remember, so long ago was it. The nature of the problem is misconceived, because many seem to think that hooks left in a pike will cause it lasting damage. Yet this is highly unlikely. I did some tests on hooks in very dilute hydrochloric acid – that is, the acid which assists digestion in the pike's stomach. The hooks were already beginning to break up in a matter of three weeks or so, and the acid I used was rather dilute compared to the maximum strength during digestion in a pike. I have on several occasions, over the years, pulled gently on a trace leading down to the throat of a pike, to find the hooks

It is a total misconception that a deadbait has to be blown clear of the hooks before a good hook-hold can be obtained. In this case the pike is well hooked in the scissors and the bait can be re-used

and end of the trace totally dissolved. Modern pikers use small hooks, and when these are accidentally left in the jaws they can be no more of an encumbrance to a pike than a few loose teeth. What is more, they seem to disappear mysteriously as though the pike is able to rid itself of them, perhaps while feeding.

Sea Fish Baits A wide variety of sea fish baits is available, either via bait suppliers of frozen or preserved fish, or from fishmongers. My own impression is that pike, in complete contrast to zander, *prefer* sea fish baits like herring, sardines, sprats and mackerel to freshwater fish baits like roach, dace, perch and chub. However, the latter baits are perfectly good baits, as are trout and eel segments, and I would not wish to discourage anyone from using them. However, another reason for avoiding roach and perch as deadbaits is that they have to be obtained from a fishery and that is another angler's loss. Most pikers use sea fish deadbaits, plus trout and eels, so this is not a serious matter. But if you do have reasonable access to roach, perch, dace, chub, bream and gudgeon, you will find that they are good baits.

Trout deadbaits are good for pike, but I have never been convinced that they are better than coarse fish deadbaits or sea fish deadbaits. Eels are under undue pressure in ecological terms and I would caution pike anglers against using them as baits. It is preferable to buy frozen eels from a reputable dealer, rather than to catch them yourself. Fortunately, a segment of eel lasts a long time, so a few packets of pre-frozen chunks are very economical.

Of the more usual sea fish baits, I list the following in order of preference: sardine, mackerel, herring, smelt and sprat. After these, I have no particular preference; I use kipper (also as small additions to the baits on the above list), mullet, cod, bass, gurnard, and even flatfish on occasion. Sardines need to be solidly frozen because they thaw out and become very soft quickly. I use them in halves simply because Tesco sardines are so large these days, and a half bait of any kind does release pleasant smelling juices into the water. Nine times out of ten I use half baits of any kind except the small ones like sprats.

Groundbait With regard to the use of fish as groundbait, there are some considerable misconceptions. The first is that by throwing in portions of fish or, indeed, whole fish, you can overfeed the pike. This is not the case. You would have to throw in crates of the fish to make an effect of this kind. Groundbaiting or pre-baiting merely provides the fish with food, contributes to their growth, and gets them used to taking your offerings as bait on the hooks. On many occasions I have caught pike with the free offerings still in their mouths – usually slices of mackerel, whole sprats or chunks of sardine and smelt. It did not stop them taking the hookbait, and in fact may well have inspired them to feed in the first place. When you remember that a pike will still pick up a deadbait even though it has in its throat another pike of several pounds, it is obvious that it is not easy to overfeed them.

Another misconception is that if the pike get used to picking up scraps off the bottom they risk swallowing the bait before the angler gets an indication and can strike. Several well-known anglers in the 1950s held this view, but they were wrong. I know, or have experienced in the past, a number of waters where the pike swallowed the bait on the spot: *none* of these waters had seen deadbaits before, nor had they been pre-baited. The phenomenon of rapid swallowing is always there and is more likely if you are fishing in a pike's lair, its hotspot: it sees no reason to move away, so it doesn't.

Another factor in this equation is that whether or not a fish 'runs' with the bait is not related to whether it is used to the bait. It is related to whether it wants to distance itself from its colleagues. Its choice is affected also by the resistance it feels from the tackle; resistance of any note actually causes it to run off in an attempt to pull the bait clear of the drag. It is not spooked by the drag, but it equates it with a prey-plus-weed mouthful, and the only way to get the prey is to pull. (Pike often hunt deep in weed-beds where they may have to pull for their supper.) Of course, if the pike picks up a free offering, it *doesn't* run off, because there is no drag and it quickly pouches it.

I have had no trouble at all with either pre-baiting or groundbaiting on the day, and I thoroughly recommend it. In fact, on club waters where many bottom fishermen fish for bream and roach, you are doing these anglers a favour, by distracting the pike from live, free swimming prey on to dead fish. Clubs ought to feed the pike this way, to the benefit of both pike and bottom fishermen. Pike which receive such a supplement to their diet undoubtedly pack on extra weight, possibly by as much as 2lb per annum in waters of high quality.

Smells Chopped up deadbaits work because of the attraction of the smell. Smells can also be added to a bait from those little bottles of oil of smelt, mackerel, and others. A tip that Colin Dyson showed me was to soak a tiny piece of cottonwool in smelt oil and then to stuff it down the throat of a smelt deadbait. The teeth of the smelt are large and they keep the cottonwool in place. The aroma is then slowly released into the water, adding to the smell of the bait itself. Another method is to tie a piece of foam to the trace and to soak it in juices. Or you can simply add a few drops to your swim. I add the

Minced fish is mixed with sausage rusk and then deep-frozen into a fist-sized ball, with a stone in the middle to make it sink. Such groundbait balls are excellent as attractors in static deadbait fishing

smell oils to a vegetable base oil which floats and spreads rapidly, and I disperse it through the swim like that. I think smells trigger off pike feeding and it does no harm to add to the natural smell of your bait.

Chopped up baits in a wire basket can also be successful. When pre-baiting without a basket one does run the risk of cormorants and other birds eating the groundbait before the pike find it. The bait in a basket can be replaced each week. Beware, however, that pike will creep up very close to the basket.

Extra smells can also be tied on to a bait. Often I add a strip of kipper, simply tied on with nylon to the body of the main bait. It seems to work very well. A whole kipper or bloater can also be used to the same effect, although it does seem rather extravagant. Another way of adding smells is to put a swim feeder half-way down the trace length with a foam insert to which drops of smell are added. Or cottonwool can be inserted into the mouth of the deadbait and the liquid smell is added to that.

Storing Deadbaits Deadbaits should be individually wrapped in clingfilm, and stored in a deep freezer. They should be as *fresh as possible* when frozen – for example, herrings should be silvery, with scales on, and have red heads. Blast-frozen baits from some of the bait suppliers are often individually frozen and do not need extra wrapping. Tesco's sardines are like this and they are very satisfactory.

Hook Rigs When inspecting the hook rigs and mountings used by other anglers you quickly detect the inexperienced deadbaiter. One of the hooks, or *the* hook if you use only one, should be located well back in the root of the tail of a bait, or in the lips of a head half bait. There are two reasons for this. One is that you want the hook or hooks to be well forward in the pike's mouth, not down its throat. The second is that if one hook is not in the root of the tail the bait casts clumsily, often kinking on a cast where distance is needed. If two hooks are in use – usually the way I fish – then if one hook is in the tail root of the bait, the other should be about halfway along the bait. It should not be more than halfway, because this may put an awkward bend in the bait, and in the event of a take such a hook could end up in the pike's throat tissue.

My preferred and most commonly used rig is the (Jardine) snap tackle, constructed with size 6 or size 8 hooks. In piking it is almost always unnecessary to use hooks larger than 6, and size 10s are not too small. My preferred brands are Eagle Claw and Alan Bramley's Partridge hooks, but for the sliding Ryder hook I have to look elsewhere: Middi do an excellent one, presumably designed by Vic Bellars.

I make up my own traces and currently use two wires regularly. One is PDQ in 20lb bs and the other Kevlar coated steel wire from Alan Bramley. Both are thicker than some of the fine wires (7-strand, etc), but they are much more

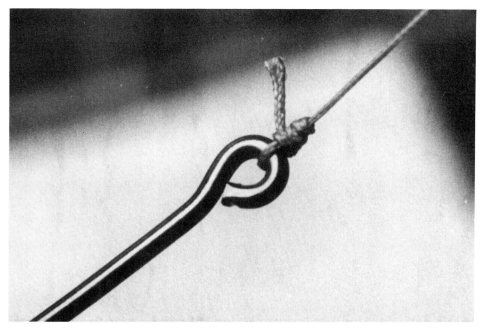

This two-turn half blood-knot is preferred by the author for tying up Kevlar and steel wire traces

supple, can be twisted up by hand (or knotted in the case of Kevlar) and are less prone to kinks. I have virtually abandoned the use of the fine wires now, as I am almost completely satisfied with the above two. In addition I use 20lb bs black-coated (plastic) wires for the upper trace, or spinning trace.

The bottom treble is twisted on as shown in the diagram, as is the swivel at the top of the trace. Before the swivel is twisted on, I slide on a Ryder treble so that it slides with a kind of stiff looseness. In other words, it slides easily enough with a push and *does not induce spiral twists* in the wire even if you slide it quickly. Hence, in a pike's mouth, spiral twists will not be induced in the wire.

I would argue in favour of a sliding treble, opposed to a *fixed* second treble, because should one of the points of either treble hit bone in the pike's very bony mouth, *not one of the six points* will move a millimetre further, unless the first point relocates itself. When the Ryder is a slider, this drawback does not apply, because one or other hook can move. When one hook slides, the three points bisect the 120° set by the other three points and you have a much increased chance of a hook point relocating in a new hold. Often you will unhook a pike, find that the Ryder has slid right down to the bottom treble, and all six points will have a hook hold. I am absolutely certain that with snap tackles one treble *should* be a slider.

Barbless or Barbed Hooks I believe that the best hooks have *micro* barbs on them, and that these are better than the common rank barb that we still see and the completely barbless types. Most anglers use semi-barbless hooks because the bait falls off if it is attached to fully barbless ones. Where it is possible for the bait to fall off, so there is the chance that the pike will fall off as well. I am aware that experienced anglers do not lose many fish on barbless hooks – indeed, I do not myself, and I have used them in trials often enough since the 1950s. Anglers such as John Watson and Neville Fickling are in favour of barbless hooks, but I feel that they are catching fish in spite of their barbless hooks, not because of them. *I have* seen lesser anglers lose fish after fish, and this can be the case especially in lure fishing where barbless hooks are entirely inappropriate for the job.

Furthermore, many anglers are leaving the runs *far too long*, knowing that they can easily remove barbless hooks from the throat tissue of the pike. Of course, experienced or sensible anglers do not do this. Barbless points penetrate much more deeply than any barbed hook, and may do so repeatedly on relocation. A barbed hook only penetrates just over the barb, and it would need a repeated heavy strike to take it more deeply – the shallow hold they usually have testifies to this fact. Deep penetration is probably unimportant with those pikers who use small trebles – they are perhaps in the majority nowadays – but I suspect that larger barbless hooks are killers because in the throat region they are capable of penetrating to the heart of the pike (this is how gut-hooked perch die, although barbless hooks are not necessary to do this in the case of perch).

Upper Trace Without exception, I always use another trace above the snap tackle itself which is on a trace about 1ft long. The upper trace is vital to avoid backlashes bringing the bait into contact with nylon, resulting in a bite-off should you get a take. Bite-offs are entirely unnecessary and can be avoided by using an upper trace (or long boom) at no detriment to the results – in fact, results are impoved by avoiding bite-offs. I use this exact rig for livebaiting too (see below), but I mention the fact here because it is obviously a good efficiency point if you can use the same rig for two differing styles. This does not necessarily apply to some of the rigs I describe a little further on.

Variations Leads can be added fixed or sliding as shown. Simply choose the appropriate weight or position for the fishing needed. I put on a sliding stop knot and usually leave it on the line even when I have no float on. I honestly think that the extra drag caused has no adverse effect on the pike. Below the stop knot I run a small bead with a bore through it little greater than the diameter of a 15lb bs line. The stop knot stops this bead, and the bead then stops the sliding float. By varying the depth to the stop knot, the tackle can be fished laying on, in traditional style, or suspended from the surface, or a lead can be used so that the float is submerged. By the addition of a weak link to either of the trace swivels, coupled with a terminal lead, a paternoster rig results which can be fished with the float either on the surface or subsurface. The diagrams are intended to indicate the kinds of circumstances in which you might use the different arrangements. Notice how, with the basic set up described, it is a matter of moments to change from one rig to another, involving at most the retying of the odd knot, or the addition or removal of lead or float.

The hook rig also can be changed. While in most circumstances I use a snap tackle as described, I might change to a single hook (perhaps a large one) if I was using sprats. And other anglers certainly use some different rigs, such as Martin Gay's sardine rig for distance casting. Other anglers use one or two double hooks as shown. In effect, these are little different from two small treble hooks, except that the particular angler prefers a single hook. One of the rigs shown was demonstrated to me by Colin Dyson (ex-Archie Braddock) and on his waters it has proved highly successful. I am not entirely convinced by single hooks, after a fairly extensive trial or two, but if the Braddock/Dyson rig proves sucessful in general applicability, then I shall change over to them, partly because I would prefer to use one hook, rather than three, as long as it works.

Some of these rigs are not unlike the so-called instant strike rig used by Alan Beat and Vic Bellars and fairly popular in the 1960s (and with a few anglers today). I have no objections to these rigs myself, but I do disagree with the arguments used in their support. Thus my rigs are as instant strike as theirs, so the title is a misnomer. One argument in their favour was that the hooks pulled clear of the deadbait on the strike. I don't think that this is important, and I often tie mine on to achieve the opposite effect. Again, I would argue that my run-to-hit ratio speaks for itself. If an angler is happy with such systems, then by all means he should use them, but I suggest that they should not use spurious arguments to support their efficiency. On the other hand, if they say that they prefer singles to trebles because they are kinder on pike, as Bill Winship does, then I can accept their viewpoint as reasonable, even if I don't agree with it.

I feel more uneasy about the use of hair rigs as advocated by Shaun Greaves, among others. Hair rigs cannot do the pike any harm, and they are just a logical extension of the principle of keeping the hook as far to the back of the bait as possible. However, it seems unnecessary because it implies that the pike, like the carp, is spooked by hooks in the bait itself. This is not the case, even on hard fished waters. When hair rigs are used, the question arises as to when to strike, I am not convinced that the angler does not have to wait too long. How can one possibly decide that the bait is in the pike's throat, and hence the hook near the front of the jaw? I will leave the matter there, as I can take it no further at present.

Belt-and-braces approach to bite indication, comprising a drop-back indicator and a line clip of silver foil

Striking and Dealing with Pike When deadbaiting I tend to use baits of 4–5oz at the most, and often much less. With the two treble snap tackle it is likely that on pick-up the pike will have the bait in its mouth with one or both of the hooks in a position to get a purchase, particularly in the scissors. This also seems to be true of the Braddock/Dyson rig. Therefore, the moment the tackle is running steadily one should wind down carefully but swiftly, then strike hard when the fish is felt. I rarely wait more than 10 seconds before striking, unless there is obvious fiddling about. Even then it pays to wind down carefully, hold the tackle taut, and then to strike hard, because the 'fiddling' can be 'swallowing'. With the rigs I use, the runs usually do run off steadily, so I rarely need to worry. On the occasions when I use a whole herring or whole mackerel, I still strike fairly quickly, certainly inside 20 seconds of getting the run. With sardines, smelts and sprats, it simply is a question of spotting a bite, picking up the rod, winding down and striking. It would be odd if this took more than ten seconds.

I don't think· it matters whether one strikes sideways or upwards. The angle at which the hooks drive into the jaw is not governed by the angle of the strike, but by the manner in which the bait is in the jaws and the firmness of the pike's grip. In theory, the sideways strike may be better, but if a fish, unbe-known to you, is facing you when you strike, then an upward strike is the one more likely to succeed.

Bite indication is clearly a critical matter when it comes to getting the strike in quickly. First, stay near your rods. Second, use a float whenever possible, because this gives the clearest indication of the initial pick-up and movement of the pike. I almost always use the same or similar back-up system whether on float or ledger tackle. For such a system, clip the line above the reel (or a bait-runner reel with the pick-up on), place the line over a rod rest with a buzzer, and have a plastic spool on the taut line to indicate drop-backs. It is a belt-and-braces approach, but it pays off with no loss of efficiency. At times of high winds, which may cause repeated irritating bleeps on the buzzer, I switch it off and watch the float and/or dropper very carefully. It is extremely rare for this system to fail to give an immediate bite indication. There are varied drop-arm indicators and varied buzzers in use, and provided these are used intelli-gently and with concentration, there should be no trouble.

A wind-beating alternative bite indicator. The plastic bobbin slides down the rod in the event of a slack line bite; and the line pulls free of the hair-grip if a 'standard' take results

The pike should be played to the net as soon as possible. Far too many anglers take too long to net a fish and it simply results in unnecessary fatigue to the pike. After lifting the fish from the water, lower the net gently on to the grass or directly into an ET unhooking net. Using both hands, press down gently on the fish until it shows signs of lying still, with no leaping and body flexing. This only takes a few seconds. The unhooking implements – left-handed glove for right-handed anglers and forceps – should be ready *before* a run takes place. Dry your left hand and put the glove on. Lay the fish on its *right* side. If necessary, kneel gently astride it on the netting, or lift it clear of the grass with your gloved left hand gripping its left jaw, and your index finger and second finger placed between the operculum and first gill rakers. (This grip should be used even if the fish is lying on the mat.)

The jaws usually open sufficiently at this stage for your right hand to hold the trace and see where the hooks and deadbait are. Normally, they will be in the scissors or fairly close to the front of the mouth. If the deadbait is still attached to the hooks and masking them somewhat, pull it clear with the forceps. Be ready for the pike to flex at this juncture, so grip the jaw firmly. The hooks can be removed then with the forceps held in your right hand. Do not put your fingers through the fingerholes in the forceps because if the pike is big and it leaps, you could easily break a finger or two. Instead, grip the outside of the finger holes in your fist.

If the hooks are further back, close the jaws of the forceps and go into the mouth through the right side gill covers. Grip the shank of the hook, release the pressure on the trace slightly, and then turn the hook sharply upside down. None of this takes long. During 1990–1 I timed the actual unhooking of my pike, and once the jaw was opened the average unhooking time was less than 10 seconds. There are complications on occasions, such as when one of the hooks is outside the pike's jaw and gets tangled in the mesh, but such complications rarely add very much to the unhooking time or problems. From netting to unhooking should be brief and careful.

Photography With regard to photography or the weighing of fish, do get everything ready before any runs occur, and also plan carefully who is going to do what. Even with photography a fish need not be out of the water for more than a couple of minutes. A little longer will do no harm, but it is unnecessary. Fish I return to the water rarely need any nursing. They simply turn upright and swim away. The object is to be successful in piking, and to ensure repeat success by handling your capture professionally.

When to Fish Deadbaits As I like deadbaiting I do it a lot, especially from November onwards. I have explained in Chapter 1 how and when pike preferentially feed on deadbaits, and you can, if you wish, restrict your fishing to

Failure to don a glove during unhooking of this fish led to him being bitten; his blood can be seen running from the jaws of the fish. Pike cuts often take several hours to cease bleeding

A lean autumn fish, to static deadbait; just at the time when temperatures start to drop and the static deadbait supersedes lures

those times of prolonged low pressure – that is, several days with a stable low. Or, if you like deadbaiting whatever the conditions, you can improve your chances by fishing shallow water in times of high-pressure regimes.

Where to Fish Deadbaits Some waters have a reputation of being poor dead-bait waters. I have never been fully convinced of this, having proved it other-wise so often in recent years. But there is no doubt that waters do go in cycles and you can have a good deadbait year followed by a year in which only live-baits or lures will work. Some rivers have a bad reputation for deadbaits, but again I have not found any of these cases to stand up to a concerted attack with the deadbaits. A few days ago Tim Cole and I fished such a river. We drew a blank on the first day, pre-baited, and got a fish of 21lb the next day.

Waters can have specific problems, such as thick blanket weed on the bottom. The trick here is to get the bait off the bottom either by using float tackle or by making the bait buoyant. This can be done with commercial buoyancy injectors which inject a strip of polyethylene foam; or you can inject air; or you can use frozen smelt which are buoyant for at least an hour if the hooks are small. An alternative is to keep a float on the surface but to remove all the leads so that the bait very slowly settles on the weed. A swanshot or two may have to be added to sink a smelt at all. The point is that there are simple ways around all such problems without changing from the kinds of rigs that I described earlier.

Distance Fishing The kinds of rods used in piking that I recommended in the previous chapter will easily throw deadbaits 50–100yd or a little further (most of the deadbaiting I have described would be carried out at less than 100yd). Further distances can be obtained by adopting beachcaster techniques and the pendulum cast, but with the kinds of rigs in use the piker is unlikely to exceed 150yd (sea anglers commonly exceed 200yd). A better way of getting distance is to use balloons, or an ET drifter outfit (or a radio-controlled boat system if you can run to such expense). I prefer the drifter rig for livebait so I will describe it in the next section. Ballooning is an art and good fun too. Avoid small balloons but choose those that blow up to in excess of 1ft in diameter (round, preferably). I attach mine via the balloon knot to a paper-clip attached to the swivel at the top of the upper trace. When the balloon reaches the required distance a strike is needed to pull it off the rig; it then bounces away across the water and countryside, until it bursts. The need for a strike is the reason I do not use this rig for livebaiting. Some practice is necessary to get the paper-clip on the knot correctly. And, more important perhaps, there may be difficulties in getting the balloon into the pull of the wind. After all, one can hardly cast it. Unlike ET drifter rigs, you do not fish the tackle on the way out, but get it into position as quickly as possible and strike the balloon off. There are some serious drawbacks to distance fishing of any kind. I would not now wish to fish at ranges over 200yd, although I have done so in the past. Takes must be wound down to and struck immediately and repeatedly – picking up the line is very difficult, and I think there is a case for a rod of 14ft in a stiff carbon blank.

Deadbaiting is a highly productive method on enough occasions to make it my favourite technique. My tackle rigs are highly efficient, provide for a flexible approach, and, provided a flexible mind is brought to bear on problems, you can succeed in most waters much of the time. There is no need to leave out a deadbait for hours on end unless it is part of a particular scheme in the downfall of a giant. As a rule you can twich them a little, or recast them every half hour or so. Or you can do this on one rod, while leaving the other rod alone. Static deadbaiting does not mean a static mind.

LIVEBAITING

The main problem with livebaiting is that it is fiddly. You have to catch and keep your bait, transport them on the day, and along the bank; furthermore, baiting up can be wet and cold in winter. Many pikers, as they get older and have a fish or two under their belts, give up livebaiting in favour of deadbaits and lures. To some extent this is true of myself. Despite the fact that livebaiting is by far the most successful method of piking, I have done very little of it for several years. However, what I do not do is fall into the trap of making excuses as so many do. I do not claim that my catches have improved during the last two years. How would I know if I haven't fished comparatively? But that didn't stop Richard Walker claiming that his catches improved when he stopped livebaiting – they may have done, but not for that reason. Nor will I claim, as some anglers are claiming, quite wrongly, that livebaiting is cruel and that other anglers should give it up, or be made to give it up. The anti-livebaiters also claim that livebaits transmit disease. As Vic Bellars pointed out in the Birmingham AA debate some years ago, there is no recorded instance of any disease having been transmitted by anglers moving small numbers of livebaits from one water to another. On the other hand, there are plenty of instances of fish farmers transmitting disease through their stocks.

Most countries make no fuss at all about livebait, and in many of the countries in which I have travelled you can buy your livebait from a shop. Big signs outside the shop tell you that the livebait is in – no distinction is made between live fish, live worms or live crayfish.

You can catch your livebait on the day, but if the pike are already on the feed this may be difficult, as often it is midwinter. It is far better to catch your

Kilty lure spoons and the now famous Flying Condom, on which Barrie Rickards has taken several 20lb-plus fish

Kilty lures, a superb range of piking spoons in excellent colours and varied weights

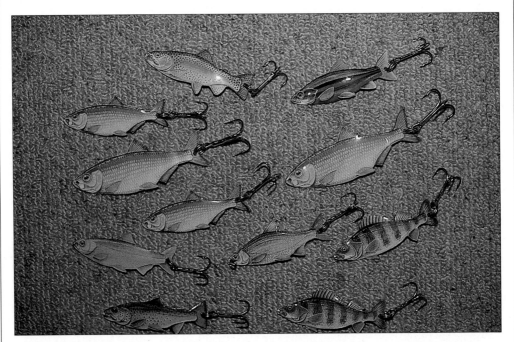

Exact imitation, as in these lazer lures, is not essential in piking; a caricature is better

Barrie's Buzzer, which has revolutionised lure fishing in the UK

livebait on the previous day, after which you have two options: either to sink it on the water in which you caught it and intend to pike fish, in a proper container such as those sold by ET, or to take it home with you and keep it in an aerated tank. The second option may be illegal in some areas, but most authorities turn a blind eye to such action and the angler who behaves sensibly regarding numbers and sizes of baits should have little trouble. Transporting containers, whether they are by ET or Shakespeare, are well designed, and the Shakespeare aerators are in a class of their own. At home a large plastic tank – as big as a bath – can be kept in the garage and aerators run from the mains. The tank should have a wire top to prevent the fish from leaping out. You soon learn how many fish a tank will hold, but one with the volume of the average bath will keep fifty 4in fish comfortably.

There has been a move among pike anglers to stick to small baits, and half-a-dozen or so should be enough for an average day's piking. So fish of 4oz or less do not impinge on the bottom fisherman's needs, and he can hardly object to the loss of half-a-dozen baits. Indeed, the average grebe removes far more fish than this in a morning's diving. This is not to say that bigger fish do not work – they do, but anglers are voluntarily giving them up in deference to the wishes of others. Bigger fish are also more difficult to use and the strikes are more difficult to hit. Some years ago I gave up using baits over 4oz and my catches did not seem to be affected – I caught just as many good fish as others using larger baits.

I would urge an element of common sense and decorum among livebait anglers. Do not keep more livebaits than is necessary. Do not carry too many on the day. Do not wave them in front of everybody, whether angler or public. In other words, be discreet, otherwise you will suffer the consequences of prejudice and misinformation. I have suggested to several firms over the years that a discreet livebait bag is needed rather than the conspicuous bait cans we employ, but none has taken up the idea yet.

Livebait in your garage tank can be fed on trout pellets and, provided you clean them out a few times each winter, they will survive. What you must be careful of is at temperature changes. If you bring home a bucketful of fish in water that is at a moderately high temperature and then put them straight into a cool tank, they will die – this is the single greatest cause of fatalities in the tank. A temperature difference of $5°$ is sufficient to cause problems. Let the new bucket of water cool down on the garage floor until the temperatures are the same. It is also very important to keep the water clean and free from dirt. Fit a drain tap to the bottom of the tank so that you can fit a hosepipe and run the water down at intervals. This flushes out waste products on the bottom and gives you an opportunity to clean some of the algae off the sides of the tank; there is rarely any need to remove the livebaits while you do this job. Simply top the tank up again afterwards. At the end of the season, remember the fish you have left in the tank. If you leave them there, they will breed if they are clean, healthy and well fed. Perch, in particular, breed quite easily. It is much better if you can place the remaining fish in a garden pond or arrange to return them to the water from which you caught them.

Another way of obtaining livebait is to buy small trout – usually small rainbows – which is widely done nowadays. Some fisheries sell them on the site, which is highly convenient to the angler and profitable no doubt for the owner. Unfortunately, such supplies are unreliable, and the suppliers rarely get up early in the morning.

Choice of livebait The best species for livebait are unquestionably small trout and small chub of 1–2oz. I used recently a 1oz trout on paternoster, and when I returned it at the end of the day it powered off up the river as if it had been asleep all day. In fact, it had been powering the float around all day. Small chub are the same. However, I would stress that the paternoster rig I describe under the deadbait section (see pp56–7) is much kinder on livebaits than any mobile rig or free-drifting rig. I normally use a livebait on paternoster for an hour or so and then return it, unless it is a trout or a chub, in which case I return it at the end of fishing.

Most species of fish work well as livebait, but some, such as rudd, tend to swim upwards and there is a risk that they will become tangled with the monofil. *Never* fish without an upper trace, which is longer than the snap tackle trace. Always fish with the gear so that it is taut from lead to float – in other words, not extremely over depth. Similarly, the line should be reasonably taut from float to rod. It should not sink in a belly so that the bait can swim over it.

Roach, perch, bream (especially small bream) are all very good baits; gudgeon, too, can be highly effective. I tend to use a snap tackle as shown whether I am paternostering dead or livebait. But there is a case with small livebaits for using two Vic Bellars hooks as shown in the diagram. When you use small baits and such hook rigs the strike should be, if anything, even more quick than when you use deadbaits. If this procedure is followed, the livebait almost always is thrown clear of the hooks and swims away, and the pike is hooked. I do not feel that the hooks need to be free of the bait for playing, but I take pleasure in the fact that the livebait is free, having done its work, and the pike is hooked.

Free-lined Livebaiting These use of free-lined and ledgered livebaits are also kind on the bait. The angler who tries out free-lined livebaiting will find that the bait swims down to the bottom and stays there. It doesn't swim about a great deal and it doesn't keep bleeping the buzzer or pulling line off the reel, which comes as a surprise to people when they try the method. Its only drawback is that it can only be used at close range, say up to 10yd. You would not want to fish at a longer range than that because the bites need to be seen very early to avoid deep hooking. It is, in fact, possible to fish at long range simply by using PVA to tie an old nut to the trace – after casting, the PVA dissolves and the tackle fishes free line. But this occurs in close-range fishing where you want to use it anyway, so distance is rather pointless. There are times when a bait fished in this way will outscore other methods – for example, when the pike are cautious and a quiet approach is wanted. You can keep in touch with the bait easily enough simply by pulling the line gently taut at intervals. This has the effect of slowly moving the bait backwards and takes may come when you start to twitch the bait up the slope.

Ledgered Livebaiting   This is a natural progression from free-lined baiting. The lead can be fixed or free running. Apart from extra distance the advantage of this method over the last is that one can maintain a very tight contact with the lead, the buzzer and/or drop arm indicator registering the slightest run, be it a full pull- or a drop-back. For both techniques the livebait should be lip-hooked so that after casting it faces the angler or lead. The runs you get are just the same as when you ledger a deadbait, but if your livebaits are rather small, you should strike as quickly as you would with sprat or sardine deadbaits. On many occasions I have had far more runs on ledgered livebait than on the more usual paternostered or free-drifting rigs. In general, I tend to use ledgered livebaiting at up to 30yd, but it is possible to use heavy leads and fish at long range. *Always* use an upper trace whether you are fishing close or far. There is a much greater risk of flip-back when you are ledgering than with other methods.

Float Paternostering   This is perhaps the most commonly used and reliable method of livebaiting. I use exactly the same rig that I would use for deadbait paternostering and the same snap tackle, upper trace and float. If I want to free drift a bait, I take off the paternoster link and adjust the stop knot to the depth I want; sometimes I add a few swan shot to just above the trace if there is a need to keep the bait down. Sunken float paternostering is exactly the same as surface float paternostering, except that the weight of lead and bait must be enough to sink the float. The only circumstances where the sunken rig is useful is when the bottom is of uneven gullies with considerable depth variations: on casting, the bait will sink and be suspended at the same distance above the bottom each time, even if you miss your target slightly. It is only a short-term expedient for me, because knowing the water depth is always a prime consideration, and I would rather have a float on the surface than beneath it.

   Bite indication with sunken float rigs is not as easy as with other methods, and the greatest care must be exercised to ensure that drop-back bites are indicated. A reasonably taut line should be used at all times. There is an argument that a normally colourful surface float is unsuitable as a sunken float because the pike might take it as a 'bait'. In fact, they take floats off the surface too, when they cannot see the colours. Sunken floats of dull grey are also taken by pike on occasion, so one cannot escape this fortunately rare phenomenon.

The surface float is an ideal bite indicator. If the tackle is set at the correct depth and tautness, then the float 'sits' on the water in a particular way. Its movements often clearly indicate what the bait is doing. For example, when a bait swims upwards, especially if it lifts the lead off the bottom, then the float tips over on its side or turns bottom up. When the bait is swimming and pulling downwards, the float shows a tugging motion which is quite distinctive. A take may also be indicated by either of these float movements, but it is a more persistent movement and often precedes the float quickly submerging. So you get an early warning that you do not get as a rule with a sunken float paternoster.

The paternoster link can be tied to the swivel of either the snap tackle or the upper trace. It tends to twist up in the swivel to a degree, or in the twisted wire of the trace, but apart from an untidy appearance it does no harm. I have tried various lateral booms, and different strengths of line, as well as three-way swivels. I do not think that any of them improve on the simpler arrangement and the tackle still seems to get twisted a little.

Leads The size of lead has changed over the years. When I first used paternoster rigs in the early 1960s it was frowned upon to use anything more than one or two swan shots. Now we use 2oz leads in appropriate circumstances and the pike don't seem to worry. I am sure that we were wrong in the past when we were obsessed with resistance to the take, because Walker and others were of this opinion.

Distance Fishing Distance with livebaits is probably best achieved with an ET drifter outfit. These can be bought in tackle shops quite cheaply, and there are clear instructions with the kits. A good choice would be one by Archie Braddock or Eddie Turner. They are rather different but both work well. I prefer the Braddock rig for its neatness, but there is little to choose between them in terms of efficiency.

When casting out tackle initially, a greater distance can be obtained than when ballooning deadbaits. But if the livebait is set more deeply than the shallow region within casting range, then something is required to make the rig travel shallow until it is clear of the marginal area. This is done by tying the bottom of the float with PVA to the swivel at the top of the trace. If a really thick knot is used, it can travel for up to 50yd before it dissolves. When ballooning deadbaits, it is not necessary to grease the line for floating, although it can be done. But with drifting a livebait out such care is vital, for if the line sinks between the float and rod, it will not only impede progress but possibly tangle with the bait and hooks. So use ET line grease, smeared liberally on the reel spool, and also in a foam dispenser tube pushed into the butt ring of the rod. As the line is pulled out (and as you retrieve it) the line is automatically greased.

Bites on a snap tackled livebait, of the bait size I outline above, should be struck immediately. With drifter fishing extra care is needed in immediate bite detection, and the very moment a take is indicated the angler needs to wind down fast and hard until contact is felt and the strike made. The very first occasion I used a Braddock drifter I hooked a pike of 21lb at a range in excess of 150yd; it seemed to take an age to tighten the line to the fish. Unhooking is exactly as described for deadbaiting; the hook rig is identical.

Large Livebaits I have no doubt that large livebaits are better than small baits when big pike only are the quarry. This is not true all the time, and I recall getting a fish of 29lb from a Fenland drain on a rudd weighing about $^{1}/_{2}$oz. There are several drawbacks to the use of large livebaits, apart from the moral question of using somebody else's sport fish. One is that although big pike selectively feed on large fish, a large livebait attracts a variety of unwanted pike. When a pike of 10lb will eat a pike of 5lb, it is no surprise that a livebait of 1lb will attract jack pike of 5lb. If you use large livebaits you only get large pike when they are almost the only fish around, or they are well on the feed, the two things not being the same.

A second problem with large baits is hooking them so that you can effectively hook a big pike should it take. Many years ago, Dave Steuart invented multi-hook rigs of careful design; these comprised two strands of trace wire leading from a dorsally positioned treble; each strand having two small trebles on it, making five trebles in all. The rig works as long as a big pike takes the bait. If a small pike takes a big livebait you have innumerable problems, and that possibility – nay, probability on most waters – means for me that large livebaits upwards of $^{3}/_{4}$lb are not worth considering. Almost every argument is against their use, save the fact that big pike do select larger food items given the chance to do so. It is not efficient fishing in my view, apart from any other questions.

Dennis Pye, who pioneered the use of large livebaits (or so people seem to think), actually used fish of about 6–8oz and occasionally 10oz. He also fished waters where almost every pike he encountered was above 13–15lb weight. That is why the method worked without the kinds of problems most anglers would have.

Pike as Livebaits I have no moral objection to using pike as livebaits on the grounds that if $^{3}/_{4}$lb roach 'belonging' to the roach angler are fair game, then so are small pike. However, despite considerable experience and success some twenty years ago, I would dismiss their use, again on the grounds of general inefficiency. I do not doubt that in waters with a few big twenty-pounders and little else they might well be a good bait, but I do wonder if, under the circumstances, a well-fished ordinary bait might succeed just as well. Incidentally, the use of small dead pike is an area that few people have tried, but one does wonder if it might be an improvement on the use of large livebaits in those waters where pike selectively feed on pike. Many waters have a cyclical pattern in which every few years the pike turn on the jack pike, possibly when the latter reach a critical density. On some such waters pike livebaits have succeeded where other baits have failed, but I do wonder whether pike deadbaits would be better still. In brief summary, avoid large livebaits as they are more trouble than they are worth.

Trolled Livebaiting This is an art which reached a peak on the River Bure in Norfolk a few years ago, although I have seen it well used on Ardingley Reservoir. The bait is set at about two-thirds or more of the water depth, beneath a float, and weighted down with a drilled bullet at the top of the trace. The bait is lip-hooked with the Ryder, and the tail treble goes in the root of the ventral fin, acting as a keel. On every water I have fished like this the retrieve speed, or rather its action, has been the same: the float rocks gently from side to side as the boat moves along. If you go too fast the float will submerge and if you go too slow the bait will drift off line. Most takes are indicated when the float simply sinks and the line pulls out of the clip. Snags, of course, have an identical bite.

Another active method of fishing is the use of spun deadbaits and wobbled deadbaits that are activated by giving them movement. It doesn't fool the fish, which is perfectly aware that the bait is dead but attacks it anyway (the matter is considered in detail in Gay and Rickards (1989)). If the pike are preferentially feeding on moving baits, they will respond to such techniques rather than to static deadbaits.

Spun Deadbaits The use of spun deadbaits is a lost art. Every time I have used spun deadbaits, especially sprats and roach, I have been successful. But it is as fiddly as livebaiting in certain respects, and hook mounts – for example, crocodile mounts – are not easily obtained nowadays. I use elasticated cotton to tie on the bait and I have a supply of various hook mounts, small and large. I usually opt for lure fishing rather than spun deadbaits, on the grounds of convenience.

Wobbled Deadbaiting Many anglers have mastered the art of wobbled deadbaiting and swear that it is highly effective. I have always been too impatient an angler to do the job properly, but despite this have had some successes,

Two spinnerbaits at the top, and a true buzzer below, with its blade spinning about an axis

mostly with wobbled sprat. For tougher baits than sprat, such as roach, a single large treble in the vent, the trace threaded through the body and out of the mouth, is acceptable. A button, bead or plastic tube needs to be placed on the eye of the treble so that the hook doesn't bury deeply into the bait. I used to use ½in diameter plastic tube, split lengthways, and arranged so that the concave side fitted over the vent region. Roach are best used gutted and the body walls stitched up again with nylon because they last longer on long casts.

In effect, a wobbled bait is fished in a sink-and-draw style, very slowly, and the bait comes in head first. Some people say that this technique is like the old trolling – for example, of Robert Nobbes – but it is not; in trolling, years ago, the bait was retrieved tail first and its nearest modern equivalent is the drop minnow technique. Another retrieve style for wobbled deadbait is a very slow but steady turning of the reel handle. In this case the wobble is effected by any slight imbalance on the part of the bait, caused by the manner in which you have set the hook or hooks. For sprats and other small baits I usually use the ordinary snap tackle, with the Ryder through the lips and the tail treble half-way along one flank. I tie the hooks on.

With sprats as bait you would think that an immediate strike would work, but it doesn't seem to. I remember once missing fish after fish on a Yorkshire drain by striking when I saw the pike engulf the bait. When a take is felt, give line immediately, and when line is taken tighten up and strike with a firm pull.

Wobbled deadbait retrieves can be slowed down so much that the method is then best referred to as twitched deadbait; if it is slowed down further it becomes static deadbait. When wobbling deadbaits I sometimes fish them static for a while and then take a break. It is a useful ploy, because there are occasions when the pike prefer the stationary bait.

LURE FISHING

All sorts of natural bait can be added to the back of an artificial lure. The first thing you need to be careful of is whether the addition will kill the action of the lure itself. Only trial will tell, but as a rough guide if your addition is much smaller than the body of the lure it will rarely affect it adversely. If something like bacon strips are added, thin strips each of less than $1/2$in wide will perform better than a wide strip of, say, 1–2in (the same applies if wool or material is added to lures).

Such additions do work. A whole perch can be added to a trolling spoon, and fish additions both small and large may help on many occasions. Bacon strips are extensively used in the USA, both with pike and other species, and many of the spinnerbaits lures come together with a soft-bodied, scented attractor. Again, these last types *do* work.

While it could be argued that a fish trailing behind a lure might leave enough of a scent trail for a pike to home in on, one cannot use the same argument with respect to plastic or material. So why do pike like such natural or artificial additions on enough occasions to make it worthwhile for the angler to use them? A clue to the answer lies in spinnerbaits, of which more later. When small pike attack a spinnerbait (or buzzer) they go for the skirt, not the blade. I have seen this many times. With big pike one cannot tell because the whole lure may be engulfed. Therefore, the pike may be *attracted* in the first place by the fluttering spoon, but when it comes to the meal the filaments of the skirt clearly have more appeal for them. In some cases they resemble

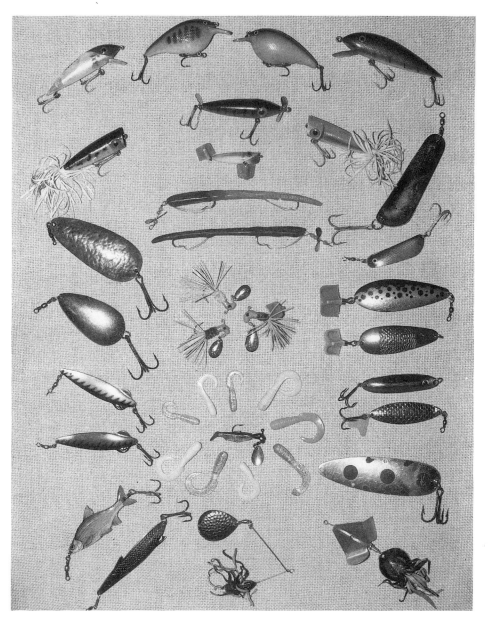

A range of important lures in the piker's armoury. The top row is made up of shallow divers, followed by a second row of surface poppers (with tassels, spinning blades and hook guards). Down the centre there are soft plastic worms with weed-guards; 'snoopies', which are lead-headed jigs armed with attractor blades; soft wobbling tails for lead-headed jigs (seen at the centre of the circlet); and at the bottom Barrie's Buzzer (or spinnerbait). Down the right-hand side are various heavy duty spoons, with a true buzzer at bottom right; on the left are two home-made copper spoons, followed by four small, heavy, slim spoons

worms; other additions may resemble fish or frogs. But it does seem unarguable that the additions to lures are what the pike chase.

This, of course, raises a very awkward question with regard to the spoons themselves. I have long believed, and have often argued, that the pike does not attack an ordinary copper, brass or silver blade because it thinks it is a fish. The experiences of spinnerbaits and lures with additives seems to confirm this. We don't really know why they attack them, but, it occurs to me that as the pike has existed for a very long time (80 million years in the case of the genus *Esox*), and as it has been very widespread in the Northern Hemisphere for all this time (for the first 60 million years in the subtropics), then its prey species must have been both diverse and ever-changing. The pike has survived so well because it *is* such a varied and versatile predator. Therefore its genetic code will hold long-buried responses, in some cases becoming fainter with time, to which it will react.

If this idea seems far fetched, let me give you an example in the form of the success of the Cisco in fluorescent red, in Fenland. We had fished one of the drains fairly extensively with a variety of lures and done moderately well on the usual 'imitations' of pike, perch and roach, when we decided to try one of Nigel Neville-Jones' Canadian Wiggly Ciscos in fluorescent red. We took about five times as many pike on this lure as on any other, and we tried others at the same time. Such a colour resembles nothing that pike are used to seeing, unless it is the stickleback in spawning livery (the male), for there are some in the water in question. They might have preyed on these when they were young. Alternatively, pike in some waters, both today and in the geological past, would have fed on charr (as in Lake Windermere today), so that the prey species may have left a genetic imprint in the genome of pike. This may explain why the pike strikes at things which bear little resemblance to its present prey. There are other possible explanations, but at the present I favour this one. So the pike is not attacking a lure because it thinks it is a specific fish, but because something triggers its 'memory' that this might be food.

Lure fishing for pike is experiencing a boom such as this facet of the sport has never seen before. However, on the bankside, very few anglers are lure fishing. I sense a change here, but not yet a big change. The reason is surely that anglers do not realise just how successful lures can be. In the last three seasons I have taken 32 pike in excess of 20lb. No less than 15 of these fell to lures. When you remember that in bait fishing one is using two or three rods, whereas on lures on is almost always using one rod, those results are good. In addition, I have had a large number of double-figure pike on lures (101 out of 211) and several hundred (about 700) less than double figures. By whatever criterion one cares to use, this is successful piking. What is more, those fish have fallen in a number of counties nationwide and in a variety of waters. Lure fishing is a prime route to success in piking.

One has to be realistic about this, however. Many anglers pursue fish other than pike in the summer months and about two-thirds of my pike on lure fall in the period from June to October inclusive. The other side of the coin is that a large number fall in the rest of the season. I write this on 5 March 1991, only two days after I landed, from a tiny drain, fish of 20lb 2oz and 6lb on a long Flying 'C'. You can expect better results in warmer conditions and this does, incidentally, apply to the winter months too – it is all relative.

Lure fishing is not a more sporting method than any other, as some writers in the past would have us believe. It is my opinion based upon years of experience that only the angler is sporting, or otherwise, not the method.

Furthermore, lure fishing, successful though it is, is not *the* most successful method. It is simply another string to one's bow, and a good one. Livebaiting is by far the most successful method, and I cannot yet make up my mind when weighing up the advantages of lures as opposed to deadbaits. But as long as you know when and how to use these methods, or as long as you enjoy using the method that takes you on the day, you will enjoy success. You will enjoy only limited success by sticking just to one method, and you will become bored.

There have been moves at times to ban, or at least denigrate, summer piking. Many years ago I was uneasy about it myself, because the pike was very vulnerable in those days in the winter, let alone in the warmer months. Today I am not worried about it at all, provided education continues as it has done recently. The point is that in summer the pike fight much harder, yet with the temperatures so high they need handling more carefully. I can say without hesitation and with total honesty that I have no trouble with returning summer pike. I tend to bully them as much as I can, sometimes heaving them over the net in a cascade of spray. I keep them out of the water for a very short time indeed, and they swim away powerfully. I do not think that pike should be put in sacks in the summer and photography should be very quick, if it is done at all.

Spinning is sometimes used as a second string method – that is, it is tried when all else fails. This is rarely the way to succeed with spinning, so you get a very poor idea of its value if you fish this way. If you want to try lures, then do fish when you think that the pike will feed. It sounds common sense, and is, but such advice is usually ignored. Having said that, it is interesting that in winter piking Tim Cole and I have found that after the baits have stopped producing you can often continue to catch on lures. Note that I said 'continue' to catch.

One of the contributory factors to the current lure-fishing boom is the growth of entrepreneurial companies which are marketing a range of lures. There are more lures available today to the UK angler than at any time in history, and by a factor of at least ten. The established companies have always had some lures, and Shakespeare have their rightly famous Big S range. But in general their ranges are small, if good, and the huge diversity available in

North America has been inaccessible. Historically too, there has been an anti-American stance taken by lure anglers in the UK, which mitigated against availability. All this changed in the 1980s as companies began to respond to anglers' needs. The two obvious ones among the early runners were TG Lures and New World Lures, which were run by fanatical lure fishermen. The ranges they have imported are impressive.

Some tackle dealers, such as Trevor Moss of Gainsborough, also have a huge selection of lures. Then there are new firms which are actually making lures, either from scratch or from imported parts, such as Simon Pearce of Pearce Lures, from whom I get all my Lucky Strike Lizard spoons. Tony Perrin produces Pikko Lures, which are among the best that are available; these I often use as double spoons which I call my Combo killers. Finbarr McSweeney in Cork produces the splendid and incomparable Kilty Lure range. I would not be without any of the lures these firms produce, and they also manufacture a good range of products.

Colour Colour cuts across lure type to a large extent. Certain colours seem particularly good for pike and I look to have a range of lures with at least several colour combinations. In fact, when I am consulted by manufacturers on lure colour and/or patterns, I try to persuade them to do a limited range of sizes, but with these colours or patterns. First and foremost I opt for any pikey colour, be it spots and bars of green and yellow or an overall colour in shades of these. I do not think it an accident that greens and yellows are good for pike, and especially something that looks pikey. Pike spend so much time eating pike that any combination of these colours is likely to trigger a reaction. Tony Perrin's Pikko spoons are superb imitations of pike, while Kilty lures do the same by caricature. I am not, however, contradicting my remarks of a few paragraphs ago. What I am saying is that while pike know that the bit of metal is not a fish, if it has the right colours, or some other important feature, then it will trigger a response and that response may be to open and close its mouth.

My second choice of colours are perchy ones. They are not dissimilar to pike colours, of course, but essentially they should be darker and with vertical bars. Spoons that wobble, and plugs, are good decked out like this, although I am less certain with spinners whether it is as important. When Ken Whitehead and I did our flume tank experiments a few years ago, it was the flash pattern that seemed to be very important with spinners (or with spoons that did not wobble slowly).

Silver, copper (and brass) are good standby colours. No doubt these simulate roach, dace, rudd and browner fish like carp and tench. Recently, some firms like Tony Perrin have put beautiful scale finishes on their spoons, which have the overall roach colour, and I have had many fish on these splendid spoons. Lazer Lures do very similar imitations of North American bait species and these are so realistic that they fool even pernickety zander. Some waters respond well to copper, others to brass or silver. In Ireland copper spoons really do succeed, and one wonders whether it is coincidence that the rudd has been for so long one of the main prey species. I know another water where brass spoons (the old Milbro Norwich spoons – that is, egg-shaped) are killers, yet in another water nearby they rarely succeed.

In addition to these main colours you need something garish, like brilliant red, orange or yellow, which often prove successful. Equally bizarre to some anglers is the use of black lures, which even succeed at night. It should be remembered that pike often see their prey in silhouette, not in full colour, in which case the prey may appear totally black. Black lures are therefore a necessary addition.

Finally, it is a five-minute job to add to or change the colour of your lure. You can turn a plain spoon into a trout or a charr, and have some fun doing so. Most firms do a trout colour/pattern in their ranges, although I have not been very successful with them.

Lures Action is achieved by the use of different styles of lure. Broadly speaking, pike lures come in the following types: plugs; spoons; spinners and jigs. Several are combinations of these, or indefinable intermediates. Don't worry about that – treat each lure on its merits and try it. But for our purposes, I want to discuss each type, and then to point to some very good lures in each type. First, get some shallow-to-moderate diving plugs. These float and rest, but on retrieve will dive down to anything from 1ft to 10ft. Shakespeare's Big S could be taken as the hallmark of this kind of lure. They can be fished close to the surface or, when fitted with a Wye lead or paternoster, can be fished in deep water. Shallow divers are easy to recognise because the diving lip is set at a fairly steep angle from the horizontal.

A few crankbaits are also a good idea. These have low-angled diving lips, often very large, and on the retrieve starting (cranking) they dive very steeply indeed. The purpose of these lures is to reach depths without the addition of lead to the line. Some of them will achieve a depth of 30ft. However, the objective is not to plough the bottom of the water, but to work the lures: you should dive them down, allow them to come up a little, then crank them down again – as you would sink and draw with deadbaits. The only time I plough the bottom is when I know that the sand or mud is clean, when the repeated puffs of disturbed sediment might well draw in a pike or two. It is not commonly realised that crankbaits can be fished in shallow water, but they can, in fact, be highly effective there. The ideal situation is when a big wind blows. Crank the bait down 6–12in, then allow it to pop up and drift in the waves. Quite a few takes occur just as the fish surfaces, and many of the takes are spectacular.

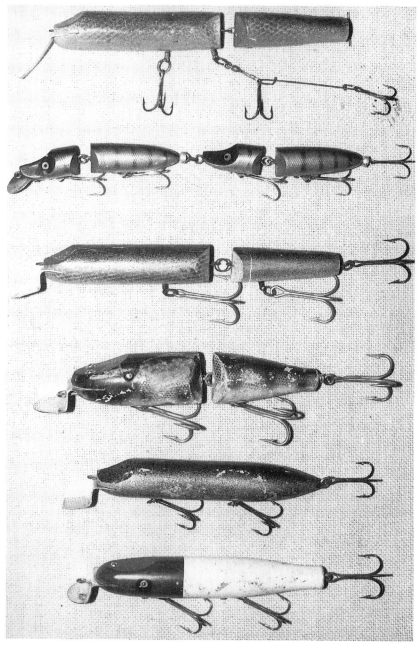

At the top is the Waddle Arse plug designed to retrieve front end below the surface, and back end waddling in the surface film. No 3 is the 'normal' version of the Waddle Arse. No 2 shows how to make a big jointed plug from two small ones. Nos 4 and 6 are Creek Chub baits and no 5 a copy of no 6, made from a broom-handle length

Remember that with all these lures you should aim to get the range of colours outlined earlier, at least as a working base to begin with. It is unnecessary to get all the colours in each range, but try to go for a mix-and-match coverage.

Lure Size It does no harm to have some big lures (say 10in), but generally lure fishermen tend to aim too big. Make sure you have a few in the 1–3in size, but mostly averaging at 4–6in overall length. It is amazing how often a 3–6in lure scores where larger ones fail. Think of the size and colour as you make your purchases.

Surface Plugs All floaters can be used as surface plugs in an emergency. However, the specially designed surface lures like the Crazy Crawler tend to be better for surface-feeding fish. The crawlers are worth a try, but so too are poppers, which come in all shapes and sizes, as well as those like the Sinner Spinner with the addition of little propeller blades. The idea of surface lures is to fish them in fits and starts adjacent to or in among the weeds and snags. It is one of the most exciting forms of piking because the take can be so exhilarating. I want to emphasise that surface lures work well, although some writers in the past have asserted the opposite. However, I would advise anglers to avoid the winter months for this form of piking because the pike are loathe to come up to the top in the coldest months, say, after October.

Spinners These lures rotate or spin about an axis. Usually they consist of a blade attached at one end to a wire axis, and the latter supports the body of the lure and trails the hooks. The body may incorporate the casting weight. The blades themselves vary in size, shape and colour, as does the body, and the treble may carry a colour tag, wool or skirt material. These are the barspoons, which are made by Shakespeare, Mepps, Abu and Rapala, among others. Veltic and Ondex are both well-known names and their products are much of a muchness; I would advise therefore that you choose simply on the basis of size, weight and colour. All the spoons vibrate well and the throb can be felt through the rod top when they are working correctly. Because pike will track them from behind before striking, a few slack line bites will occur on barspoons. Unfortunately a slip of weed has exactly the same effect. Even so, every slack line effect must be treated as a take, and a sweeping strike is needed to take up the slack.

There are other kinds of spinners, such as mackerel spinners, minnow and quill minnows (now of plastic); in effect, these are *tubes* which rotate about the linear axis, helped by a couple of small blades. All spinners twist up the line to some extent and if you plan to use them for more than ten or fifteen minutes, I would recommend the use of an appropriate-sized Wye Lead at the head of the trace. These will effectively kill any tendency there is to twist, and they assist casting at the same time.

I have done extremely well on barspoons and spinners over the years. My two best fish that have fallen to them recently were a 24$\frac{1}{2}$lb on a Sonic Rooster Tail and a 20lb 2oz on a 6in Flying Condom, the latter being a cross between a barspoon and a minnow. In the small sizes it is indubitably a barspoon. Each spinner has its day and its water – for example, the underrated mackerel spinner is perhaps incomparable in shallow water or water where the weeds reach almost to the surface. It can be fished extremely slowly.

Spinnerbaits Spinnerbaits are not really spinners, but a small range of them is essential. I deal with them in detail later in the chapter, but here I simply wish to indicate that they are neither plug, nor spinner, nor spoon, nor jig. The weighted body with its inturned single hook is plug-like, adorned by a skirt; the blade is a little spoon but set some 2–3in away from the body on the extremities of a V-shaped wire. Spinnerbaits vibrate as strongly as barspoons, but unlike the latter the tassel is offset from the spinning blade. Some of these lures are essential in *any* lure bag. I fish them both shallow, with a sink and draw motion, or very deep either with a steady retrieve, or sink and draw. Where the bottom is known to be clean, they can be twitched very slowly along it.

Spoons A spoon is a spoon-shaped blade. On retrieve they wobble about an axis, rather than spin, unless the speed of retrieve is faster than the designer intended. Hooks are attached at one end, as a rule, and a split ring and swivel are attached at the other. So there is no wire axis, or even a hypothetical linear axis, because the spoon darts and wobbles its way to the bank. Furthermore, a spoon does not twist the line up like many spinners.

The essential varieties of spoon are three. The classic egg-shaped spoon, which is convex on one side, and concave on the other, is usually termed a Norwich spoon. In Ireland it is referred to as the 'copper and silver' spoon. It is also the spoon that results if you make your own from teaspoons or tablespoons. For details regarding colour and size, see pp80–1. I restate this to remind you that spoons need not be just silver or copper. Indeed, the best stables like Pikko and Kilty provide pikey, perchy, roach-like and mackerel finishes.

The second type of spoon is an elongate version of the Norwich, which is perhaps twice as long for the same width; it is usually called a Vincent spoon, after the Norfolk fisherman Jim Vincent who used them for trolling on the Norfolk Broads. The Lucky Strike Lizard which I detail later in this chapter is just such a lure. Of all the spoons this is my favourite, and in general I prefer Vincent Spoons to either Norwich or the third type, the Toby.

The Toby is a trade name, and other firms do similar, slim, concave-convex

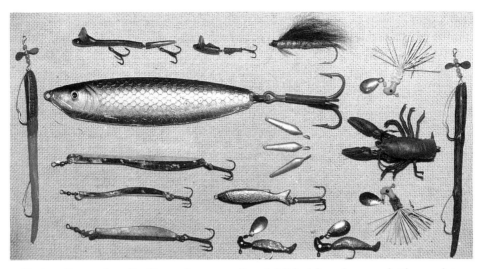

Various jigs, perks, pike flies and worms, all useful fished from boats or bridges and, in suitable swims, from the bank. The crayfish is a weed-free lure useful in river piking or used as a jig when boat fishing

lures. These are for distance casting and deep water, par excellence, but the smaller sizes can be used to effect when the pike are fry feeding. Most of these lures will spin if they are retrieved too quickly. They also have an unusual attribute, – namely, that they can be brought back *extremely slowly* when the bottom is snag- or weed-free, and yet the action remains true. This is because they operate well from a very slow wobble to a very fast wobble. Most other spoons have a single, optimum, retrieve rate which you need to know about. I have never been as successful with Tobys or their equivalents as I have been with Norwich and Vincent spoons, and it may be that they *do* have an optimum retrieve speed which is a little too fast. This is quite likely as the Toby was designed originally specifically for trout and salmon fishing.

Jigs These lures are allowed to sink and are then jerked upwards by raising the rod tip. Some of them look like plugs, others like spinnerbaits; they do, in fact, transgress classificatory boundaries. The point of attachment for the link swivel is largely what determines their jigging action. These are little used by UK pikers, which is a pity for I have had many pike on such lures. Of course, all spinners and spoons can be pressed into service as jigs, especially when boat fishing, but jigs are designed to have a good action when they are fished in this way.

Other Lures There are spoon plugs of at least two styles, made of metal. In profile they look like plugs. Blade-runners are currently the most famous, but

Gudebrod Sniper (top); Lucky Strike from Pearce Lures; new Kilty lures (bottom)

the US spoon-plug, which was once rare, is increasingly available. Others are mixtures of spoon, plug, spinner and fly – for example, the fly spoon. I would recommend always having a few odd-ball lures in your bag for those days when all seems dead, or for those waters that have seen it all.

Favourite Lures There are several lures that I would not be without under any circumstances. Top of the list, beyond any question, would be the buzzer or, as it is more correctly named, the spinnerbait. In my opinion, it is about three times as effective as most other lures. It does look very peculiar with its Y-shaped wire frame, attached blade and inturned hook with skirt. My two favourite skirt colours are black, and chocolate and orange. The best weight is $^{1}/_{2}$oz, and I think the best blades are either egg-shaped and beaten copper, or willow leaf and nickel. Combine these with the two skirt colours above and you have perfect combinations. However, colour being so important in piking, I would not hesitate to ring the changes if I thought it necessary.

Buzzers are usually taken confidently and it is rare for them to be followed to the bank side. This in itself is a bonus when lure fishing. Furthermore, a pike will come repeatedly at a buzzer if it misses or falls off. This may be related to the overall soft nature of the bait, for the pike grab the skirt, not the blade.

There is the additional advantage that the buzzer can be fished through most weeds, except blanket weed, as well as through thick lily beds, sunken trees and snags. However, the single hook can cause the fish to come adrift, so when the water is known to be snag-free, I attach a treble hook to the single. This is achieved very simply by pushing a piece of valve rubber or plastic tubing over the eye of the treble so that a tight fit is made. Then push the point of the single through the rubber and treble eye, finally working the treble around to the bend of the single hook. Fish rarely fall off this rig. The waters where the buzzer is ineffective are few, and as a rule lure fishing is slow on them anyway. In the last few years I have taken five 20lb fish on buzzers, as well as a great many other fish.

The next great lure on my list would be the Lucky Strike Lizard in copper and nickel finish. This is a long Vincent-style spoon with a slow, rocking wobble. I have taken five twenty-pounders on it in the last few seasons. Mine come from Pearce Lures in Minehead, and I usually buy him out of stock at the annual PAC conference in Loughborough. It was this lure that was responsible for most of my 800lb bag that I took in a day and a half in 1989. It is probably one of the best lure-caught bags of pike on record, with 80 fish, an average weight of 10lb, one of 22lb, and 23 over 10lb. The Lizard can be retrieved just below the surface for it sinks slowly, but it is just as good at depth. Its sink rate is less than 1ft per second – the $^{1}/_{2}$oz buzzer sinks at a little over 1ft per second, so both are easy to count down to the working depth.

After these two lures the rest are in no preferred order, but I rate them all as exceptionally good and very versatile. Tony Perrin's Pikko lures are superb, especially as you can get pikey, perch and roach finishes in two weights of metal. They all cast well and Tim Cole swears by the lighter version. I usually arrange Pikkos in combination – that is, two spoons in tandem with a mid-way as well as a tail treble. when I do this the perch colours are my preference, and I use a smaller spoon as the lead spoon. The result in the water is an unusual plug-like wobble and a most effective lure. It casts very well; yet it can be fished just below the surface if needed.

The Kilty stable is also top class. My favourite is the 7in Heron, which comes in a range of colours and patterns. This is not a distance caster, but is fine for rivers and drains and for trolling. The surprising thing is that it takes pike of all sizes, despite its huge length. On retrieve it has a very slow rock from side to side.

From the same stable I am also keen on the heavy Norwich or egg-shaped spoons with the mackerel or pikey finish on them. These are for distance and depth and are good for reservoir fishing or the big, deep gravel pits. I also use the red Flying Condom in the large size. This is a kind of barspoon, but with a long body reminiscent of the old wagtails. It casts like a bullet, and has a vibratory retrieve which pulls the rod tip around. The overall length of the large version is about 6in and it can be fished either deep or shallow. My first fish on this lure, after about ten minutes' fishing on a small drain, was 20lb 2oz.

Plugs I would rate two plugs as about equally successful – namely, Shakespeare's Big S and the K12 Kwik-fish in coachdog finish. The big S is a good general lure, which is always likely to produce both small fish and large. The K12 is a bigger, jointed plug which wriggles like a short eel. It sinks extremely slowly due to the weight of the trace, or it just floats. Hence if you stop the retrieve it 'hangs' in the water. Should it be followed by a pike, stop the retrieve, let it hang, then twitch it forward. The result can be electrifying. I have had three twenty-pounders on the K12 as well as plenty of other good fish.

I would also recommend the Creek Chub range, especially the 4in shallow divers, and the 10in three-joint version. The smaller lure can be fished very quietly. It may be my imagination, but the old wooden ones seem to land on the water with less of a splash than the plastic ones. Beneath the water they are equally effective. Each has produced several twenty-pounders for me.

The following list completes my prime choice of lures, although it must be said that I am constantly trying them out as I see likely winners in catalogues: Timber Rattler (silver); Crazy Crawler; Sonic Rooster Tail; Ryobi's Mugger and Troubleshooter; floating plastic spoon; Gumpy jigs; Rapala floaters and Fatraps; Shadrack; several crankbaits; Blair spoons; Kuusamo spoons; Squidgy Rubber Jobs (I know not their names); Veltics and Vibro barspoons.

TRICKS OF THE TRADE

First, I shall assume that you have a bagful of lures and the lure fisherman's kit that I discussed in the preceding chapter. Secondly, I shall preface further remarks by saying that there is no point in stinting on lures. If you have fifty in the bag you will lose none at all; if you have three you will lose two. Furthermore, there can be no doubt that a selection of lures will give you a chance of picking up the colour, size or action needed on the day.

Ringing the Changes One of the first tricks of the trade when fishing for pike is to ring the changes. I change my lure every five minutes or so, sometimes more frequently, in an attempt to pick up the taking bait. It can be that critical: a slight colour, size or action change and you catch ten pike. Fail to detect it and you get none. Be suspicious if you get follows to the bank and no takes.

It can often be almost impossible to make a decision about what is necessary. It becomes a matter of trial and error, and your past experience on that water. As a general rule I opt for dull lures on a bright day, and bright lures at dawn and dusk. Yet black lures can succeed well at night while on other occasions a gaudy orange is taken despite bright sunshine.

If we explore this area of doubt further, it becomes obvious why we cannot compute the combination of colour, size and action. First, consider the water colour. It may be clear, coloured brown or green with algae, or brown with suspended silt. As the depth changes so does the light value, especially in water with any colour. Then think about the ambient light. Even if the sun is not shining the water will always be lit from one direction; but that direction changes during the day as the sun goes round. Then even nearby waters, or different parts of the same water, vary in the angle of the bank to the light direction, and that also changes during the day relative to other positions. This can mean that pike will be chasing one colour in one part of a water and another somewhere else. So one really *must* be prepared to change lures frequently. I begin usually by relying on my past experience of a water, and try to take into account not only the time of day and the swim, but the overall weather conditions and water colour. Although it can be a hit-and-miss affair, you do build up a store of experience which helps to cut the corners.

Casting Techniques Try to fish in such a way that the retrieve is effective for its whole length. If you are fishing a small drain for example, try to cast close to the far bank, not only for the fish that may be under it, but to get the bait down to working depth before it reaches the centre of the drain. There is no point in getting the depth, speed and action correct just as you are about to lift the lure from the water. If you do this you may well get an unnecessarily high number of 'follows'.

Always try a cast or two along your own bank, particularly before you walk along to the next swim. But on small water try to avoid very long casts along the water. It is much better to creep along making short, quiet, effective casts.

Pike often take first or second cast through a swim, although there are exceptions to this, such as when you are using small, relatively inconspicuous baits. These non-spooker baits are the ones to use on small waters or waters which you wish to search slowly and carefully – as, for example, when the temperature or pressure is down and the pike might be expected to be sluggish in response. If you are fairly certain that you know a good pike-taking spot, perhaps from previous visits, then avoid walking straight up to it and chucking the lure in. Try a few casts which land, say, 10yd from the expected taking area, *then* put a cast on its nose. It will have heard the plopping of the bait going in, and this will have had the effect of getting it worked up and ready to strike.

I am strongly opposed to the casting round-the-clock routine advised by many writers, past and present. Try to cast where you think the pike are. There is a case on occasions for systematic searching of a water, it is true, but it makes for boring fishing and it is best avoided when possible.

Fishing in Weedy Waters Fishing the weeds and snags I deal with elsewhere in this chapter, with reference to specific lures. But the following are general tricks that you can try in shallow weedy waters where the weed comes short of the surface. One of these is to fish a float in combination with the lure, a method rarely seen, but deadly at times. For example, a heavy spinner or spoon may get you well out over the fish, but you may be unable to retrieve it far before it sinks deep enough into foul weed. The trick is to use a long trace with a float on it. If the depth of the water over the weed is, say, 3ft, then use a 3ft trace with the float set 2ft above the lure. You can use an ordinary sliding float and peg it with a piece of twig. The float needs to be buoyant enough to more or less support the lure. The lure cannot now sink 3ft down. The reason for putting the float on the trace is that the pike in such waters do take the float as well. You can put a hook on it if you wish. In deeper water, where a float and lure combination can also be used, this is less important. I use this method with both barspoons and plugs (floaters *and* sinkers). Think about its versatility: you can do not only the above style, but can float a plug down a river, under trees yet above streamer weed, and on the retrieve the plug cannot dive into the weed.

Covering the Water Almost the opposite of the above technique is the paternostered lure. Here a perfectly ordinary paternoster rig (not a float paternoster) is set up and a floating plug is the bait. When the lead hits the bottom, the plug floats upwards so that its distance above the bottom is the length of the link, plus the length of the trace. As you begin the retrieve the plug dives, and you can stop it diving as far as the bottom by varying the retrieve speed. You can also fish sink and draw. The great advantage of this method is that you know exactly how and at what depth the bait is fishing.

The float and lure technique described above is used with what one might call 'normal' lures. A slightly different use is to have the float as a former – that is, its main purpose is as a casting weight. In this case tiny lures can be cast a long way. For fishing them deep, however, it is necessary to revert to the paternoster or to use a sinking former. In the last instance the former need not sink quickly and, indeed, might float before the addition of the lure. The important point is that is should be heavy enough to cast. These 'floats' should be made preferably of heavy wood and streamlined to help the retrieve. I 'borrowed' some of Bill Winship's ordinary pike floats as they suit this purpose admirably. They have a peg at each end and attach by a rubber sleeve. By adopting these various tricks we are able to cover the water, and cover eventualities the more easily.

Night Spinning Pike feed often at night and one of the most useful tips for night spinning is to tie a stop knot about 10ft up the line above the lure. As it clicks through the tip ring on the retrieve, you know exactly where the lure is. On small waters where you wish to avoid hitting the other bank you can set out the required length in daylight and, with the line out in the water, put a rubber band over the spot. Each cast will then stop at the rubber band, but a pike will be able to take line from it. It takes a little practice to master the technique because you do not want the line to work out gradually as you fish. Aim to fish shallower at night so that the pike can easily silhouette the lure against the sky.

Using the Drop-off There is another circumstance, this time in daylight, when it is useful to silhouette the lure. This is where there is a sharp break in the slope from the shallow edges to the deep water – the drop-off, as it is called. Pike often sit at the foot of the slope or part-way down it, watching for fish swimming along the top of the drop-off. Then they come and have them. They have a murky background behind them, camouflage beneath their bellies, and the prey probably don't know what has hit them. Drop-offs are not only a feature of big waters and boat fishing – they occur on all kinds of water. It pays to cast *along* them and to bring the spinner back just over the top of the break in the slope.

Guarding the Trace Another tip which is of general application in piking, but which is most useful for the lure fisherman, is to guard the twisted end of the trace with a *blob* of glue. I emphasise the word, 'blob' because a smear still allows the weeds to catch up on the trace. A blob slides beautifully through all the weeds, with the exception of blanket weed or silkweed. Araldite is perfectly satisfactory for this purpose, but I find it messy myself. So now I use a little Bostick gun which melts a blob of plastic at its nozzle. This solidifies beautifully on the trace, much more quickly than resin, and does the job well.

The Retrieve Lure fishermen argue intermittently about the type of retrieve necessary. In fact, the matter is perfectly simple. Most lures have an optimum speed of retrieve which brings out their designed action best. Generally, you should stick to this, at least to start with. As a rule, this means a steady retrieve. My own experience confirms that a steady retrieve, which should be close to the 'correct' speed for the lure, is generally more productive. If you use a long rod for lure fishing, then a different action can be imparted to the lure with relatively minor movements of the rod tip. Should your rod be short, say 5ft, then the same action can only be obtained by much greater wagglings of the rod tip. I think this is why short rod anglers always appear to be so frenetic.

4

THE BIG FISH
WATERS

If you want to give yourself the chance of catching a giant pike, a fish upwards of, say, 25lb in weight or, better still, several of these, the first thing is to keep your eyes open and your ears tuned to where you might find one. Press reports may provide you with relevant information. Many people heard about Ardingley Reservoir, in Sussex, a few years ago through the press; they visited the reservoir, asked about the swims on arrival, and for some lucky ones this resulted in fish over 30lb in weight. Of course, if your read about a good fishing venue in the press, so will thousands of other anglers and your fishing will be competitive (to get the best swims) and crowded whether you get the best swims or not. Ardingley was as crowded as any trout reservoir is during the trout season, which was appreciated by the owner at the time.

Occasionally you will see an article in the press which will tip you off, but which other anglers may not notice. However, this type of article usually applies to smaller waters such as large gravel pits, which you were probably aware of anyway. Local angling columns may be more useful in this regard than national angling newspapers. Information obtained in this way is more likely to give you good pike rather than giant pike.

Possibly a better system is to gain knowledge through the grapevine. There is an effective grapevine running through the big fish world, and waters with giant pike in them rarely remain secret for long. Therefore, attend meetings of your local pikers, or NASA, and go to national meetings too. You can obtain information by talking to people and writing to them. As a rule you will draw a blank, but every so often you will come up with a big fish water. The disadvantage of this approach is that if the grapevine has leaked the news to you, it will have done so to others.

Let me give you an example. Several seasons ago a good friend of mine, Eddie Turner, made some remarkable catches of thirty pounds plus fish from a southern water. I knew of that water, from a sideshoot of the grapevine, several years before that! It happened that there was no way I could take advantage of the knowledge, so I had to leave it as a possibility! At that stage very few knew of it. Similarly, in 1989/90, the Lake District's Esthwaite Water began to produce very large pike. The potential was always there, even many years ago

Many big lochs, lakes and loughs are strewn with boulders, not only at the water's edge but well offshore. Avoid any technique which lays the line along the bed of the water

when large roach and hybrids were being captured regularly. Those people who knew about the fishing early enough made quite a killing, but after a while angling got a little crowded and one feels it will decline before many seasons are past.

As a general rule the objective of the pike angler who wants to make his killing should be to find out early, catch the fish early, and to move on to pastures new. *All* information that reaches *you* on the grapevine is also reaching others. In this chapter we are discussing big waters, because they at least do have a few years' life in them even after general discovery. For example, if you take Loch Lomond, or Corrib or Mask or Ken or Ree, you can still catch good pike there. The waters are, if you like, too big for the fishing to decline very quickly. Small waters of, say, less than 20 acres, last about a season under heavy angling pressure. The medium waters – for example, Ardingley and Esthwaite – may last for two or three seasons with luck. But they do all decline, in a variable time-scale, the smaller waters quicker then the larger ones. The decline is caused entirely by overfishing. Therefore the pike angler seeking success by this means of common knowledge must be thoroughly hard-headed and move on sooner rather than later. And before he moves on he will have enjoyed, or not, somewhat crowded fishing, a competition for swims, and always some aggravation.

The next way to consider catching a giant pike is to concentrate on certain very large waters. I mentioned several of these in the last paragraph, and one could add to the list the Broads, Hornsea Mere, several large trout reservoirs and numerous other Irish, Scottish and Lake District lakes. These waters have a long-standing reputation. They have survived, in a fashion, both overfishing and official pike culls. But they are very difficult and the fishing is slow. Nevertheless, it is often peaceful fishing in attractive surroundings and the rewards can be in proportion to the work put in. I think if I was personally interested only in fish of 30lb upwards, I would do this kind of fishing, rather than chasing the medium-large and the small waters, with their invariably short-lived periods of excitement. I do fish the giant waters occasionally, still, but it is as much for the atmosphere, and the change, as it is for the possibility of giant pike. One could lose one's common sense by concentrating on such waters. For example, in the mid-1960s Richard Walker tried to sell the idea that Loch Lomond would produce real giants of 40lb plus if enough keen anglers fished it regulary. They did. Lomond didn't. Indeed, it has not produced many 30lb plus fish. The reality is harsh in the world of giant pike. Slog it out with the ever-moving crowds, or slog it out with waters of almost unmanageable proportions. But for success to follow, it is as well to appreciate the reality.

Notwithstanding all the problems that might be described as natural, that face the would-be piker, there are also unnatural man-made problems. Some of the trout reservoirs which harbour enormous pike also beset themselves with rules, ostensibly designed to protect the trout. The number of rods may be restricted, together with the baits, the fishing hours, the fishing days, and so on. So this particular tack is in many ways the most irritating of all. I don't mind the natural restrictions – size of water, the weather, competition from those who thought of it first – but I do object to being allowed to fish in a very restricted fashion, so I don't do it. In time things will change as trout managers realise that pike present little threat to their trout stocks, and they will need the income from tickets. At the moment they can call the tune, but it will not always be like that. The trout managers are also slow to realise that the keen pike man is not interested in his trout, either to fish or, by and large, to eat. If he can devise methods to avoid trout, he will do so.

For those who have decided on a large pike attack on some of the big waters, I should like to use Lough Ree in Ireland as my first example. First, you should write to the Irish Tourist Board and the Central Fisheries Board. In 1990 Graham Marsden, the famous Cheshire specimen hunter, had a very large pike on Lough Ree, so if you have contact with him, or an introduction, you would write for his advice. This is the art of the information-gathering technique. You may not always get a response, or the response you get may be unhelpful, but you have little choice. Even enclosing an SAE may not help, but you should always do so anyway.

Netting a big Lough Allen pike which tested the tackle to the limit

Then you will need an Admiralty Chart of Lough Ree. This can be obtained from HMSO, or you can buy one in Dublin at large stationers or boating chandlers on the quays. A chart is vital, and you should never go afloat without one. I usually contour mine, in colour, just to make the spot heights (depths) clearer. You can then add your own notes to it as time goes by, greatly enhancing its value for future trips. One of the first things which becomes apparent on looking at the chart is that Lough Ree is not a deep lough. There are areas over 100ft deep, but a great deal of it is much less, and many areas have a very pikey depth of under 30ft.

Matters like accommodation are relatively straightforward in Ireland and you can find guest-houses at good rates. You can also camp and cater for yourself more easily and, indeed, in somewhat better surroundings than in the UK. Ray Webb did this for quite long periods, although for most keen anglers a week at a stretch would be long enough, most especially at times of soft Irish weather. So the would-be Ree piker has to decide on a base camp. This might be Athlone in the south, which also gives easy access to quieter loughs when conditions are bad – for example, Killinure, Coosan and Garnafailagh. Alternatively, Lanesborough on the northern end might be chosen, perhaps giving a greater chance of more varied boat hire. Or somewhere down a western or eastern

shore might prove preferable. All this depends on your own views about how to tackle a big water, such as beginning by facing the prevailing south-westerly wind direction, a tactic adopted to start with by some anglers. Or it may depend on information you have obtained about where big pike have been caught in the past. Always remember, of course, that big pike of the past, and to a degree of the present, are dead; you cannot specifically go looking for repeat captures, as you might on a moderate sized water in the UK. I have a preference for the southern end of Lough Ree, but I have also had good (but not giant) pike in the north and west. The east side looks better in certain areas, more particularly where the River Inny discharges in the lough, but I have no experience in that region, other than on Inny itself.

The next stage in the proceedings is to talk to local pike anglers or to local game anglers who catch pike accidentally or occasionally in matches. Foreign tourists, including those from the UK, may help a little, and they do have one advantage over the locals in that they know what you mean by big pike. My own experience is that many Irishmen will tell you what they think you want to know, rather than be very factual. This is because they want to share your enthusiasm; it is not an attempt to mislead in any way. To other Irishmen any pike is a big one (as well as a dead one) and the information will often be general rather than specific. You can also contact the Northern Irish Pike Society (NIPS), although their collective expertise might be on other big waters such as Lough Allen; and I believe there is an Irish Pike Anglers' Club based in Dublin.

You need to collect, assiduously, information from all possible sources, and then to make judgements as to its value. Often the information that you store away proves to be the most important. As an example, I was informed several times in my questioning that a perch added to the rear treble of the trolling spoon actually improved the taking rate of the system. It seemed unlikely to me, as it was outside my own experience, so I noted it as a 'belief' and temporarily forgot about it. Later I was to change my mind completely on this matter; and I also now know that the trick has widespread effectiveness.

In the past boats could be a great risk, and when Charles Morley and I fished the western shores of Lough Ree we only had boats with sponge bottoms. Every hour or two we had to beach to empty out the water. Today, things are much better and anything from a Shannon longboat to a cruiser plus dinghy is possible. I have never used a cruiser myself, but I would do so, because I like the idea of comfort with efficiency. In the past I have slept many times in an open longboat, or camped nearby, and it is a splendid way of undertaking a fishing trip (see also Chapter 6).

First, you will need to forget about the hundred-feet depths. Most pike are found in water shallower than 30ft or so, against breaks in slope, where rivers enter, or where weed-beds grow or fringe the area. You should look for these. By all means think about water from 40 to 50ft, and run the graph recorder

George Higgins of Northern Ireland with a 25lb lure-caught fish from Lough Allen

over such areas, but you need something positive to go on because you are fishing what I call the great unknown. Physically, it is difficult to fish very deep water and perhaps it is only worth trying when fish have been 'sighted'. In my experience, on Killinure Lough, itself rarely over 50ft deep, good pike do come from about 40ft down, especially south-west of the island.

In the spring the pike may be in the side loughs and in the shallows. Even well into May very big pike can be found in the extensive shallows that fringe some of the bays. There is something exciting about alternating trolling the drop-off itself, perhaps against reed and bulrush beds, with drifting over heated shallows looking, bepolaroided, for basking giants. Some of the crucial areas are where the sunlit shallows, perhaps less than 2ft deep, give way to water 4–6ft deep, where weed and reeds afford ambush and shelter. Some very big pike indeed lurk in these regions – they have one eye on the sunlit shallows and one eye on the drop-off.

The question of technique itself is no great problem in theory. Basically, I would be inclined to troll on the echo-sounder, using a downrigger system (either commercial or homemade). For baits I would use various plugs, spoons or spoon and bait combinations; while in shallower water I might troll a dead perch or trout on its own. This can be done on the outboard engine if it is a good one which allows you to troll slowly; or with an auxiliary electric motor such as the Shakespeare model I use; or on the oars. A word on trolling on the oars: in Ireland they are not usually in rowlocks, but on the much safer thole pins, so that in the event of a take the oars can be 'dropped' and picked up again at the appropriate time.

My objectives would be first to try those areas to which I had been directed by local knowledge or by other information and secondly to use my own common sense. Some areas simply shriek pike at you and it would be foolish to ignore these. Other areas are pikey because they are of easy access and regularly fished; their productivity may be on a very irregular basis, barely enough to keep alive their reputation. So do not be afraid to try something new on Lough Ree.

On locating a pike or two on the troll I advise throwing over a marker buoy immediately. Where one pike exists the chances are that there are others or even a hotspot. The marker buoy should have a float, the wherewithal to coil sufficient line about an axis on it (it can be dumb-bell-shaped) and it should have a heavy weight to uncoil the rope as it sinks, spinning the buoy as it does so. After that you can keep on trolling past the buoy at various depths or, if feasible, you can anchor and fish towards it with lures or with baits.

I can vouch that these tactics work on Lough Ree, and that they will work for all pike. The question of catching giant pike is down to three further points: a) assessment of past captures; b) gut feeling about the nature of certain terrains; c) luck. The last of these may be the most important – that or persistence.

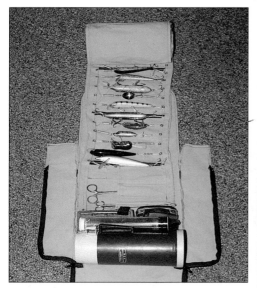

Most lure containers, whether box or bag, result in extraordinary tangles during the course of a day's fishing – especially if enough lures are carried to ensure success. Barrie Rickards has designed a lure bag which carries all the usual tackle but unrolls to hold up to 30 lures without tangling, *hence saving much time and temper*

Correct method of unhooking a pike. Note that the mouth opens without use of a gag. The pike could also be laid on the grass and the same technique employed

Barrie Rickards and Colin Dyson with pike to 27lb

Bruce Vaughan spinning in thin lily beds. With the Buzzer in use much more closely spaced lily beds can be fished, often to greater advantage

Malcolm Bannister with a grand pike set against the grandeur of the Scottish highlands

If we move to Scotland and consider Loch Lomond, it will demonstrate one or two features of giant waters, if not of giant pike. My results here have always been fairly good, but as in Ireland I cannot boast a 30lb fish, only catches in the mid-twenties. To some extent some of the logistics are similar: no licence is needed; do you choose the north or south end?; do you go to Balmaha or Ardlui, or Luss in the middle, or to the enigmatic east shore? Accommodation is a matter of hotel, guest-house or caravan site, because camping cannot be pursued in Scotland with the freedom it can in Ireland. Cruisers are a possibility, though. The water is deeper than in Ree, but that only gives you more areas to dismiss (at least provisionally). The same features harbour pike, or have concentrations not far away, namely, river entry points, weed growth, drop-off and, at some times of the year, extensive shallows. But in Lomond more than in Ree it may be more valuable to understand the movements of migratory fish. The big pike certainly feed on their runs, especially of powan, but whether they ambush them or follow them I know not. You will find an equal number of experienced anglers who take one view or the opposite.

Local information on pike will be less easy to obtain, because in Scotland, unlike Ireland, there is generally a loathing of pike. The Scottish are either not interested in them, or dislike them. The Irish have always had a sneaking regard for pike and an admiration for the pike hunter who would forsake brown trout for them. Not so the Scot. So the information you obtain on Lomond is more likely to come from the English grapevine and a specimen hunter than it is from Scotland. It is, however, true that there is a growing number of Scots, still small in number, who are interested in pike, and many of these are found fishing Lomond (or Ken). Their ranks are listed in the branches of PAC in Scotland. A contact with the PAC Secretariat will be necessary.

The Lomond Admiralty charts are good, and everything else logistical is as in Ireland, except that the boats are better and well maintained. The techniques themselves can be the same, but there is more bank fishing on Lomond than on Ree or on the many other Irish big waters. So the angler who is simply unhappy in a boat, or afraid will find bank fishing at Ardlui and Balmaha, even if it is a little crowded at times. There are other bank spots too, and there are still some to be discovered. But, as always, a boat gives you better access to bank fishing. (You can also tow the baits out, and groundbait by boat.)

In my opinion, plugs seem to be more effective on Lomond than spoons, which generally I prefer to use on Irish waters. Equally, the trolled bait and bait-plus-spoon seem less effective, whereas static deadbaits seem a little more effective. I may be wrong about these factors, but I do recall that static deadbaiting was good even in the early days before any deadbaits had gone in as groundbait. In Ireland, and most particularly on Ree, I would always drift my deadbait off the bottom, under a float. There are enough exceptions to these generalisations to make anything worth a try. Under certain circumstances I would anchor up and cast my lures on Lomond, but I have found that less successful than straight trolling along a specific contour. The circumstances where I make exceptions are where I have located fish close to the drop-off or on the shallows. On one occasion I took fish after fish on Balmaha shallows on plug, when I was anchored in only 3ft of water. It was on Balmaha shallows that I also realised the value of the Sniper plugs for slow wobbling in front of the pike's maw. It is a pity that these are not widely available, if they are available at all.

Hornsea Mere in East Yorkshire is another big water, but it is not as large nor with the same pike potential as the Irish and Scottish big waters. It does, however, throw up 30lb fish from time to time and as its fettle has looked good for a while, perhaps there is the possiblity of a few more. Nowhere is this water more than 11ft deep as far as I am aware, so it is one big pike swim. On the other hand, nowhere are the pike more difficult to find. I have certainly found them more easily on Ree and on Lomond. There is a little bank fishing which can be good at times, such as when the huge roach shoals congregate around the boat jetties. It was from here that Eric Allen made his legendary catches in the 1950s, and the club stalwarts of those days (Harold Blackburn was one who is still around) did even better, though more quietly. Hornsea will certainly come back – big waters with a reputation always do.

The boat fishing is easier today in one single respect, namely, that Mr Hood's boats are good. In the old days the non-club members used a kind of punt, like a big coffin. Boat fishing is not easy on this water, although it gives access almost everywhere except the bird sanctuary at the western end. Trolling does not seem to work too well, perhaps because much of the water is too shallow, but trailing a float with suspended deadbait does work. If this method is pursued at the same time as someone is casting a lure around the boat, then concentrations may be located.

Instead of positively pulling a float behind the boat, one can allow the wind to drift the boat, control its angle to the wind with the dip and tilt of an oar, and let the floats follow behind. This causes the hull to disturb the water before the float reaches it, but in a quieter way than positively pulling it. The baits can be set at different depths, and this method is easily operated by one angler. From my experience on Ree, Lomond and Hornsea, the passage of a boat hull over their heads does the pike no harm at all with regard to feeding. Often enough it seems to have a positive, rather than an off-putting, effect.

On Hornsea Mere perhaps the most crucial factor is that the pike especially the big ones – can be very tightly packed into small hotspots. I have uncorroborated evidence that in recent years the hotspots have been in the bird sanctuary. Given the inability to identify the hotspots, the next best thing is to try to hit the Mere on the best day during the best conditions. As on all other waters this would be on a high pressure rise, particularly at the very beginning of what turns out to be a prolonged or steep rise. You cannot know that easily, naturally, but the thaw after a freeze-up is something to watch for. The actual thaw may take place on a falling barometer, but a day or two later the winds go mild, from the south-west, and up goes the barometric pressure. As a result, the pike may go on the hunt with abandon. I have recently had four twenty-pounders in one day under such conditions, so they really are worth watching for. A south-westerly wind on Hornsea pushes the water to the boat-house region, and whether a thaw is underway or not, the roach shoals may move there too.

On the other hand, one cannot often be fishing when the pike are on. If you miss the crucial period by half a day, you will miss out completely to the extent that you might feel that no pike were in the swim; when you have experienced the before and the after, it is sobering to think that so often you are fishing above good fish which have no intention at all of feeding.

However, if you manage to find a hotspot, a very brief feeding spell every day would be the norm. This might be half an hour to an hour and a half, but you must be certain to be there. For some weeks it will be at more or less the same time, to more or less the same bait, and to the same method. The substance of these observations was originally made on Hornsea Mere by Ray Webb and myself, and we recorded our findings (Webb and Rickards, 1971).

Bosherston Lake in Pembrokeshire where many principles of lure fishing were worked out in the 1950s by Clive Gammon

We could only fish part of a hotspot because in those days it was on the sanctuary boundary, but it measured a maximum of 30 × 20yd. Within it, 30 × 10yd was prime. Occasionally they left the area on a feeding trip, and turned up all over the water. On other occasions they will congregate if vast roach shoals congregate, or when gathering for spawning. And in contrast to Lomond or Ree, their presence might be the more easily detected in view of the differences in the scale of the waters themselves. When you are afloat on Hornsea it seems huge, but one is never overawed by it as one is on Ree or Lomond when the storm clouds gather. The waters of the Norfolk Broads are more homely with respect to particular swims, or stretches like the Bure, or some of the individual broads. The piking is probably more difficult than on any of the foregoing waters and the pockets of big pike are more scattered and 'secretly' located. But they have a reputation and a history of piking second to none in these islands. Here, thirty- and forty-pounders do occur, and there are big twenty-pounders for the skilfully persistent.

I have fished the Broads for longer than many of the current generation of experts, but very intermittently and in recent years only rarely. For these reasons, I do have a real appreciation of the achievements of anglers like Fickling, Turner, Hancocks (both), Watson, Wilson, Amies and others. They would be the last to deny that giants are there for the taking, but the first to make the point that their taking is a giant effort too.

So if you wish to follow the road to giant pike in a satisfying way, I would urge you to make your pilgrimage to the Broads. Some of the worries of the very large waters actually disappear. Or, to put it another way, you can be as bold as you wish or as tentative as you like. Troll a spoon down the boat channels as the Vincents did; or work a livebait in the manner of Pye against the Norfolk reed-beds. But you can also troll a small livebait or a deadbait beneath a float, on the River Bure; or you can bank fish static deadbaits on the river or mere; or you can spin from an anchored boat. Perhaps the Broads are all things to all pikers, except for deep waters and truly mountainous seas. Even tidal-water piking of exceptional quality is available.

It is, perhaps, this very range of successful styles that caused some individuals to concentrate on one style only. Pye would rarely be seen without his dumb-bell float; the Vincents trolled Vincent spoons; Giles and Sandys ledgered static deadbaits (in part, certainly, because others said it didn't work and they are a stubborn pair); Holden plugged or wobbled deadbaits (only leaving them static while he had his lunch); Wagstaffe and Reynolds cast all manner of ironmongery from an anchored boat; and so on. A little later, some anglers decided that versatility was the key, and then Fickling and Watson, among others, came along. But each and every one of them caught thirty-pound pike, even forty-pounders, and sometimes more than one man deserves in a lifetime.

5

DECADE ON A GRAVEL PIT

Colin Dyson

By fortuitous means, around a decade ago, I 'inherited' a large gravel pit. It was not unknown to the pike angling fraternity, for a few keen and serious anglers had fished it. They had behaved themselves and had been tolerated by the local sailing club, which had sole rights. Then someone unwisely publicised the fishing, in an over-dramatic manner. It was trumpeted as a water which possibly held a forty-pounder and, worse still, there was a photograph which proved to be a major clue for those who obviously tried to find it.

They succeeded; the banks were suddenly crowded with new anglers who did not have the sense to adopt a low profile with the sailors, who called in the local police. Pike fishing was suddenly a back number. The police could fish if they kept everyone else away, but the police didn't have a pike angler in that branch of the force. What they did have was a resolute frontman called Terry. Waves of applications for permission to fish broke over him: phone calls, letters, even an application to conduct a 'scientific survey of pike in an unfished water'. But nothing moved the man.

While all others were failing, my fishing companion John Austerfield worked on an ingenious scheme. A certain peer of the realm he happened to know was friendly with directors of the company which owned the gravel pit. It led to permission to fish a pit nearby, with a friend, and it proved to be one of the easiest doubles waters in Britain. The 100-acre pit holding this wonderful forty-pounder, however, was as far away as ever.

For myself, I took the same route as hundreds of others, but I got a different result. Terry, it seemed, was an avid reader of *Coarse Angler* magazine. He 'knew' me, even though we had never met. It snowballed from there; we are now great friends. If there was one stupendous perk above all others which derived from fourteen years I spent editing that magazine, then that was it. I grew to love that pit. A hundred acres for the exclusive use of two pike anglers, who were later to be allowed the privilege of taking their friends. The only problem in the beginning, though, was that I actually didn't know anything about gravel pit fishing. Furthermore, I was not even a regular pike man.

I had enjoyed the glories of the Broadland fishing as a novice in the 1960s, and found it difficult to come to terms with other forms of piking. It all seemed second best after the Broads, and for more than a decade I had just played at the game. I had had a few twenty-pounders on occasion, from Yorkshire rivers and Lincolnshire drains, but none of my previous experience was of much use on a gravel pit. With hindsight, I know that what I lacked was not so much the basic methods, which were easily learned, but the 'feel' for the place. In most of my other types of fishing I had a fair knowledge of my quarry and how they should respond. I could 'think' like a fish, but I couldn't think like a gravel pit pike for a long time.

I hesitate to say that I can do that, even now. Gravel pit pike are predictable only in their unpredictability. In a decade of non-stop learning the biggest lesson I have absorbed is that when a successful method is found it is time to start looking for another. What is working may work that day, that week, a few weeks or the whole season, but it won't work for ever.

Don't misunderstand me. Any bait and any method will always catch pike, but to achieve consistently good results on pits you need to be versatile, constantly trying something new. That knowledge came as a shock, for I had thought that is would be easy to catch big pike from a pit which was now totally unpressurised. In the beginning, however, it was anything but straightforward. The pike had, of course, been conditioned by what had gone on there before, but they had had a year or so when no fishing had taken place. I thought that they would have forgotten the dangers inherent in baits, and I certainly thought that two anglers and their friends could not possibly pressurise a 100-acre pit. I am now totally convinced that the opposite is true, for the more successful we ultimately became, the more short-lived were the productive methods and baits.

To give a few examples of how things change, from the start we discovered that ledgered mackerel, half mackerel and herrings were almost useless as baits, which was hard to believe. Probably they had been heavily used by anglers in the past, but we persisted with them on at least one rod. In the first two seasons I got only four runs on mackerel, although they were all good fish. Perversely, a visitor came with John and got nine runs in the day on mackerel, an event we are still trying to understand.

Some pike anglers criticise the use of more than two rods, but I have a conviction for doing it. In many places it would not be acceptable, but it is a different matter when you are alone fishing 100 acres. We have persistently used several rods solely to test baits and methods, but when we found something which worked we never switched all the rods to it. To my mind that would be unacceptable and, indeed, rather boring.

Almost always there is only one rod apiece employed on what we have found to be the best current method, and almost always that is the one which

A variety of pike floats on the author's workbench – including converted Fishing Gazette
bungs – and the balsa rod from which many pike floats are made

catches. Occasionally, something we are trying out produces a fish, and possibly we are on to the next leading method. With two rods it would have been impossible to have the luxury of one, almost useless, mackerel rod, for that is what it was for about six years. It seems that it took that long for the pike to forget mackerel. We had odd good fish on them, including several twenty-pounders, but in the main it was like watching the proverbial paint dry.

The change, when it finally came, was dramatic. Three seasons ago, at the time of writing, mackerel suddenly became more productive, catching several fish over 20lb for me and others for friends. Herring came into its own at around the same time; in fact, half herring alone has caught me eight fish over 20lb in the last two seasons. To be more exact, I actually caught sixteen twenty-pounders altogether in that time, but this was towards the end of a long learning process, and the fishing overall had improved as a result of a management exercise that had been carried out some years before.

From the beginning, we quickly learned that the best way to catch pike was to livebait, using a simple sunk-paternoster rig or drifting one around on a float. We gave various deadbaits equal time, but almost every time that the indicators fell off or a float went down, it was a livebait rod which was in action.

We were not, however, catching many big pike. The place was swarming with small pike and probably had a small number of big fish. I began to see why Nev Fickling, one of the previous regulars, had never caught a pike between 7lb and 22lb. There was a dearth of doubles, so much so that John actually caught two over 20lb before he got one between 10 and 20lb. Naturally, I told him that my eight doubles in that first season was the greater triumph.

I should have kept quiet, for the following season I had only five doubles from that pit in twenty-seven visits. A more sensible angler would have gone elsewhere for a while, but they had been decent doubles, including my first twenty-pounder from that water, and those mythical forty-pounders might just have been somewhere there.

To return to the subject of baits and trends, after a while we noticed the live-bait runs tailing away on the sunk paternoster rig, a pike-fishing version of a tackle that Vic Bellars had designed for perch. I worked out a way to improve it, taking the bait further away from the sunken float, so that it could not tangle, and giving the bait more freedom to swim.

The effect was dramatic. We were getting far more runs than we had ever had before on an SP rig, and I believe that was the first lesson I had had on the need to ring the changes when something has stopped working well. That particular change was merely marginal, presenting a bait with more swimming area and a little higher in the water, but there was something about it which either appealed to the pike or, perhaps, failed to deter them. Maybe they had become wary of a bait working in close proximity to a dark ball.

Eventually, the new rig became ineffective too – or at least much less effective. Whether it was the rig or a change in the behaviour of the pike I am not sure, but over several seasons the effectiveness of the livebait was steadily decreasing, no matter how they were fished.

Bearing in mind the experience of that rig change I started to fish livebaits in different ways. One way was simply to ledger them on a standard deadbait rig, mounted the 'wrong' way round. That caught some fish, including a memorable capture.

I had cast a small chub livebait out on a 2oz bomb, waited a few seconds, put the rod in the rests and started to reel in the slack before fixing the indicator. I was pulling in slack with the left hand and winding it on to the reel with my right. But I seemed to be doing it for an extraordinarily long time. The line wouldn't tighten. Had the bomb swivel broken? Had I found a great hole of previously undiscovered depth?

In fact, I had just thrown the bait straight at a big fish, which had taken the chub on the drop. Then it had swum so directly towards the rod tip that I was in acute danger of winding it straight down the rod rings. When finally I tumbled to what was happening and struck, the pike was in the shallows under the rod tip. There was about 4ft of line between rod tip and pike, and it used all of it to jump into the air. I must have flipped off the anti-reverse by sheer instinct, which was fortunate, because a fresh 23-pounder on that short a line would be lost nine times out of ten.

I believe that the pike probably showed some preference for different species of livebaits, or at least they seemed to respond to something different. In the beginning, we mostly used perch and skimmer bream, which we both found easy to obtain. Small chub, when we first got hold of some, were much more effective, as were dace. For some strange reason, however, trout have proved quite useless. Several anglers have tried them, but I cannot recall a single run.

Barrie Rickards added to the evidence that doing something different works. The very first time that he was invited to the pit he fished a livebait that we had never used before, a sizeable rudd. I told him to cast it into a deep corner, where we had taken a number of good fish. Within the hour he had added nearly 3lb to what was then our pit record with a very long and lean fish weighing 27lb 4oz.

Barrie Rickards' catch was an interesting fish. I had caught it four years earlier, in our second season, at 17lb plus – it was easily recognisable because it had a missing ventral fin. It was damaged in the battle, when one of Barrie's hooks broke a gill-raker. It was an unfortunate incident, but not the disaster that many pike anglers believe it to be. On its return, the pike, which clearly had not fed for a while, went on a feeding spree. I was to catch it half a mile away, only six weeks later, when I was fishing in the dark. It then weighed 30lb 12oz, but until I checked the photographs and saw the missing fin and the body markings, I had thought it was a totally different fish. It was very fat and solid when I caught it, and had clearly not suffered any disadvantage from its broken raker. Another big fish in the pit, which was caught much later by Pete Haywood, had a broken raker dating back before our time. It was in superb condition and weighed 26lb.

Fisheries scientists have decreed that pike never learn about livebaits, because they are such a natural food item. That may be the case, but I certainly think that pike learn about the ways that livebaits are presented. There has to be some reason why our livebait catches declined between 1982 and 1990–1. I went from catching three doubles on livebait to every one caught on deadbait, to a situation in 1989–90 when every double fell to deadbiat. In 1990–1 I had twenty-three doubles, with only three caught on livebait.

What had been a slow decline in the effectiveness of livebaits actually became a crash-dive in 1989–90, for the previous season, when I did more fishing than usual, I caught twenty-seven doubles on livebaits and twenty-three on deadbaits. The statistics may be a little distorted because in both of the last two seasons we gave up fishing livebaits half-way through. They weren't catching and we didn't want to kill fish for nothing. Had we persisted, however, I doubt that the figures would have changed much.

Whether this trend will continue I cannot say; I have learned to expect the unexpected. I hope it does, however, for we have enjoyed the battle of wits using deadbaits in various ways. We have done almost everything you may have read about elsewhere, and possibly other things as well.

Our dyed deadbait experiments led us nowhere. The experiments started after I had had a disaster in my livebait tank, when I lost about thirty skimmers when the pump stopped working. I dyed the fish a golden colour and put them in the freezer. For a long time I could not catch a fish on them, but John Austerfield bagged up. He caught pike on over twenty of the golden skimmers before I had caught anything at all. I dyed another batch of fish gold (without telling John) and was fairly successful with them. Straight ledgering them worked, but suspending them on sunk paternoster rigs was better. Popping them up worked well too.

The skimmers were almost the colour of rudd. In the summer of 1990 I caught some ornamental rudd in a carp lake, and one died in the keep-net. I froze it for use as deadbait, and it was fished as a pop-up several months later. The near blood-red fish accounted for a 22lb 2oz catch, my first pike of the 1990–1 season, but I was not able to repeat it.

Curiously, red was a colour which never caught one fish for me in other bait-dyeing experiments, although some anglers claim it to be a good and effective colour. However, my 'Arthur Scargill' red baits were no good at all, and neither were my 'Maggie Thatcher' blue baits, the colour fish are supposed to see best at depth. Again, blue has worked for others. My 'David Steel' yellow baits have caught a number of fish. What we learned from all of this was that gold baits were taken often enough, but in the beginning they had not insured me against the normal 'swings and roundabouts' results that can be expected when fishing with friends. The chances are that John would still have out-caught me during that particular spell if the baits had not been dyed.

The success of yellow baits over blue and red ones suggests the exercise of preference by the pike in certain conditions, but I do not think we learned anything conclusive. When we stopped using dyed baits, the deadbait runs continued at much the same rate. There was never a moment when I began to think that we were on to something which demanded further examination, although I still dye an occasional batch of fish gold. During 1989–90, gold roach produced pike weighing 19lb 12oz, 14lb 8oz and 12lb 8oz, and a gold scad caught a 25lb 4oz.

These baits were all fished as pop-ups, and in the same period an equal number of good doubles fell to undyed natural deadbaits fished in the same way. Nothing is proved by this, except that golden baits do not deter pike. The method mentioned here, however, is worthy of further comment. Within the period in which mackerel and herring were making their comeback, there was a spell when popped-up naturals – mainly roach or hybrids – were catching nearly every pike we landed. I shall explain what we did and why, so that you will have an idea of how you can think your way to a few good fish.

We were having a lean spell towards the end of the 1987–8 season, when nothing was producing more than the odd fish. Archie Braddock, who is a very useful angling companion, began to experiment with unleaded livebaits, float-fished about 4–6ft deep over deep water. He caught a few, mostly small, pike; generally the bait was driven to the top before it was taken. The method is still worth a try in slow spells.

One day, however, he lobbed a bait out and it swam determinedly back towards him. A pike was following it. We watched, spellbound, as the pike, which weighed about 7–8lb, followed the bait over the drop-off and into the shallows. The bait beached itself in trying to get away, and the pike stopped, no more than a yard away. It eyed up the bait, flipping around on the sand, then turned away, lazily picking up a dead fish which had been dropped in the margins earlier in the day and disappeared back into the deeps.

The incident made Archie think. We had two paternostered livebaits out, and he wondered whether pike were looking at them without taking them. We hung on deadbaits instead, and one of them caught a pike. That set Archie thinking even more, and over the remaining weeks of that season we embarked on an approach which combined his two discoveries – that the pike currently wanted natural deadbaits instead of livebaits, and that when nothing seemed to be happening pike were catchable high in the water. However, although he had caught on livebaits high up, we wondered whether they would take deadbaits popped up far higher off the bottom than they were commonly fished.

After some experimentation, we decided to use super-buoyant baits – balsa rodded, air injected and, in the case of bigger sea baits, which we also used, a polyball stitched to their noses. The ledger weights were made into links, designed to allow the line to run through with complete freedom. I made a type of stand-up ledger with a PTFE curtain-ring at the top end. The ring was too wide for standard beads to be used as a stop between link and trace, so I used a 1/2in polyball instead. Archie opted for a big ledger link bead at the top of his bomb link, with a 1/2in polyball on the link line to make the rig stand up. Although the rigs were different, the result was the same.

We would cast and leave the bail arms open, allowing the heavy bombs to plummet to the bottom. The baits would either stay high up or surface a few seconds after the bombs had hit the bottom. We always knew the depths in which we were fishing, of course, and we could simply wind the bait down to any chosen depth. Usually they would be wound right down to the bomb, where they were popped up only to the length of the trace.

From there they could be lengthened a yard every few minutes. Sometimes the bait would be released altogether and rise to the surface, hopefully catching the beady eye of a passing predator. It was, for those few weeks, not exactly a deadly approach, but it caught when nothing else would. My last three doubles of the season, weighing 11lb 8oz, 13lb 10oz and 17lb 10oz fell to the method, and Archie did even better.

We were ready with this method the following season, but it accounted for only very occasional fish until after the turn of the year. Then it was bonanza time, starting on 8 January 1989, when my diary shows I caught two different fish of 14lb 4oz. On 29 January it caught me one of 19lb 12oz and another of 16lb. On 12 February I had catches of 14lb 4oz and 13lb 3oz. On 19 February I took a 14lb 8oz catch, then one of 25lb 4oz; on 26 February I took one of 12lb 8oz. I never caught one double on any other method during this spell. Archie's results were similar, and they included a different 25-pounder which actually took a popped-up bream off the top in 18ft of water. Archie had just cast in, and was preparing to wind the bait down.

We caught those fish at all depths, and very often above half depth. For six weeks those pike wanted a bait in no other way, and Archie had also found that the method was exportable. He was catching with it as Staunton Harrold, a very big and hard water where totally unproductive days are more common than catching days. Nobody else seemed to be catching, and he appeared to other anglers to be doing nothing different from them. They were all ballooning baits a long way, but his was performing in a very different way once it was there.

It is an abiding mystery as to exactly why the catches suddenly started on 8 January and why they ended on 26 February. It was almost embarrassing, for we had told John the method when he came down to fish in the last couple of weeks of the season. We also told Pete Haywood, who joined us for a day, and he was not best pleased. If mackerel became extinct, Pete would have to stop pike fishing, and the news that mackerel baits had been ignored for six weeks was far from welcome.

We were discussing the situation on the day that the pike had mysteriously lost interest in pop-ups, but were keen on mackerel, eels (which had never worked before) and sand-eels (which had never been used before). The season ended in a flurry of twenty-pounders on mackerel and sand-eels, and a handsome collection of doubles on eels and sand-eels. Much to Archie's disgust, I signed off the season with two twenty-pounders in a day, one of 23lb 3oz caught on a sand-eel, and another of 22lb 2oz caught on a mackerel.

If anyone could understand why these things happen, and could accurately predict them, he would become the greatest pike angler in the history of the sport. Our pop-up method did not work at all the following season. Sand-eel has not worked as impressively since, although Archie did catch a 25-pounder on it last term.

When netting a hard-fighting pike for a friend get in position early, keep a low profile, and sink the net before the fish approaches it

If you fish gravel pits for long enough, you will have a head full of methods and approaches which have worked at one time or another, and which have to be tried again. Take fry feeding, for example. The pit produces fry in vast quantities every year. During the summer great shoals of little fish patrol the margins, but in only one season have we encountered pike which were interested in fry feeding. I wish we knew why, and I certainly wish we could experience it again.

What was to prove the most hectic spell we have ever enjoyed on the pit began on 23 October 1986. I had arranged to see John and a pal of his, but for some reason I had slept in, Having calculated that I could not get there before 10am, I decided to work instead and to go early the next day – what a mistake that turned out to be.

John and his friend fished the south bank for most of the morning, working their way to the south-west corner, where I had intended to fish. When I didn't appear, they decided eventually to fish it. They had 11 doubles in my swim, including one of 21lb, two of 19lb and a 17-pounder. Every fish, they said, had spewed up vast amounts of fry but, curiously, all their pike had taken ledgered deadbaits and, to make me feel worse, they hadn't started to catch until noon.

Next day I failed to catch on either live- or deadbaits, but I did pick up a couple of low doubles on a Kuusamo spoon. I also picked up a very strong feeling that I should fish the swim again the next day. The fry were still there and I had seen a few good pike 'humping' on the surface (hence the spoon, although with hindsight a small spinner might have been better).

It was rare to see pike topping on that pit, and it was over 20ft deep where they were doing it. I went prepared to fish spoons and spinners up top, but it was sunk-paternostered lives which did the trick. I had a catch of 20lb 8oz on a perch, four other doubles on perch (two), roach and a gudgeon, and one on a spoon. They had all been on the fry, but the biggest double at 14lb 10oz, was stuffed with them. It disgorged fry throughout the fight, filling the swim with screaming, diving gulls, and it threw up just over a hundred little bream in the landing net. I counted another hundred floating around the swim, and many had been eaten.

I was also surprised to find that while some of the pike had bream in their throats, others had only perch fry – none had a mixture of the two. I was catching them all in one small area, but learned on the next trip, six days later, that the fry-feeding was occurring along about 100yd of bank.

I was fishing with John and we spread out. I caught a 24lb 8oz pike on a Kuusamo Professor – my biggest pike on a lure at that time – one of 20lb 9oz on a livebait, two 17-pounders on livebait and one of 10lb 14oz on a spoon: in all I had caught three 20-pounders and eleven doubles in two trips – it was unheard of. A week later Barrie Rickards caught a 27lb 4oz pike, a 15-pounder and, I believe, another double or two. He also caught one of 16lb 8oz on one of my rods, because I was playing a 20lb 12oz fish at the time. I went on to make a 17lb 13oz catch and a small double. It all ended when a gentle westerly wind gave way to a strong south-easterly blow.

Not only have we never repeated that fantastic experience, but we have never caught another pike with more than the odd one or two fry in its throat. I had 'wasted' a day in that three-week spell, incidentally, trying another corner I knew to be choked with fry. I caught nothing at all and, rightly or wrongly, concluded that virtually every big pike in the pit had been in the south-west corner

It was a mystery why, with fry available everywhere, they had packed into one small area and how they had all known where to go. Could it be instinct, or a form of communication that is not known about? It is held by carp anglers that when fish are caught in certain ways on certain baits the other fish can learn about it. It isn't necessary to catch all the fish on a bait or method before that bait or method is discovered. My experiences with pike on my pit seem to point in a similar direction. We simply cannot catch all the pike in the pit; we frequently see fish we know we have not caught before. It would not be possible for any method to become suddenly useless unless all the pike made the same decision – those which had been caught on it and *those which had not*.

If there is a pheremone-based warning system via which fish react to chemicals emitted by other fish which are injured or frightened, then it is in order to wonder if they can communicate other information in the same way. Can pike tell each other that 'the girls are bagging up on bream fry in the south-west corner'? Or are the fear pheremones emitted by a vast shoal of fry detectable from a great distance?

This is, of course, intriguing speculation, but there are so many other possibilities. I am on safer and more common ground to mention the more obvious fact that the behaviour of fish is influenced by water and air temperatures, atmospheric pressure, wind directions, light values, and so forth. We have known for years that all these factors influence whether and how enthusiastically the pike will feed, but do they also affect their choice of food? We exchange information with anglers fishing other pits in the region, and it is uncanny how often we find the same things. When we were catching almost exclusively on natural deadbaits the same was happening on the other pits. When their fish are on sea baits so, as a rule, are ours. Even the actual species of sea bait which is working best is often the same. It happens too often to be coincidental; pike are more complex creatures than we are sometimes led to believe.

Location is a key issue. We began by fishing swims we knew had produced big fish for others, plumbing around and learning the features as we went along. Later I was able to map the whole pit, using a graph recorder which confirmed our early, painstaking findings and showed us the whereabouts of every submerged island and sand bar. The depths run to 26ft at normal level, but average at about 14ft.

We have caught where there are no obvious features, but fishing to features is preferable and more productive. The most important feature is the near-bank drop-off; it is certainly the biggest at around 3 miles in length. Slopes from islands, channels between sandbars or the edges of sandbars, areas which travelling fish would have to pass to get from one part of the pit to the other, fry concentrations (watch the gulls and grebes), any bump on an otherwise flat area, sunken machinery or other snags, corners, inlet pipes, temporary pipes pumping water from other pits – all are important features or situations to consider.

I have stopped worrying about weather conditions. We have failed in what have seemed perfect conditions and caught in appalling weather and through holes in the ice. I don't like easterly winds, and rarely catch when they are blowing. Strong northerlies aren't much better, but when the odd fish does show in these conditions it is very often big.

We haven't found the eastern bank to be any more productive than the west, south or north banks – in fact, the reverse is true. Others, including Eddie Turner, when he was plundering thirty-pounders from his chalk pit, have enthused about the east bank possibilities, and I do not challenge their findings. Pit fisheries have a lot of common rules, but some have different characteristics.

Our pit has permanent, transient and seasonal hotspots, and we try to fish them in a sensible manner. We rest swims for weeks and sometimes months. We move when we start to see too many recaptures. Were the key swims fished more heavily, or occupied all the time, as they are on some waters, maybe the fish would move and find sanctuary on the east bank. I may decide to rest every bank except the east one for a whole season, just to see what happens.

The most effective hook rig to emerge in the past two seasons is one developed by Archie Braddock from an idea of mine. It uses two Vic Bellars doubles on a 20lb wire trace. It seemed to me that I got more runs on that rig than I did on small trebles, and I put it down to the fact that pike could not feel them. They would flatten to the body of the bait when the bait was mouthed.

The success rate on the strike seemed as good if not better than on trebles; my diary shows that it was very long time before I missed a fish. For some reason, however, I drifted back to using trebles, perhaps because as the editor of *Coarse Angler* I was frequently given samples to try out.

Archie had been catching a lot of Trent carp on hook-out rigs, and wondered if something similar would work with pike. He experimented with my rig, sticking the rear double into the tail root of a deadbait and lashing it at a 90° angle to the bait with elasticated cotton. The hook is then kept at the correct angle when a frozen bait softens because, of course, it remains tight. The front hook was simply latched in, in the normal way.

Archie went through the 1989–90 season without missing a single run from any size of pike. I had a terrible spell losing fish on a rig made with a size 8 and size 10 trebles. Four big fish came adrift in a short time, so I changed to his rig. I missed nothing for the rest of that season.

One interesting fact which emerged from the exercise was that almost every pike was hooked in or close to the scissors, and every single time it was the lashed hook in the tail which was engaged. The other usually remained in the bait which, more often than not, was hanging outside the pike's mouth. Clearly, we had a very 'fish friendly' rig. The only problem we had was with one fish early in the following season. It was hooked in the regulation place on the lashed hook, but the other was stuck fast in the gill-rakers. We had been relying on the second hook (which was changed to a big single in the second season) to hook any pike we might strike with the other hook outside the mouth, but it never seemed to happen.

I took the plunge and removed the second hook. I switched to the Marvic Specialist double, which is stronger in the wire than the Partridge VB. A few small fish fell off in the second season, but we have landed dozens of fish on that rig. The success rate was as near-perfect as we could have wished; and we never delayed a strike. I would be disappointed if other anglers adopted this rig and fished it with any lack of confidence. Detect the run, wind down and hit it. You will connect at least as often as you will on two trebles, and probably more often. And the unhooking will be simplicity itself, with no damage to your fish.

I started to use big doubles. The smallest I use is a 6 (the biggest of the two hooks on the double, of course) on such baits as smelt. I use 4s on herrings and mackerel, and even 2s sometimes. They are just as effective. The rig is a supremely efficient hooker of gravel pit pike, and the original rig with two doubles is suitable for livebaiting (one hook for small baits).

I could not understand for a long time why Archie's rig worked so well, for it breaks some of the rules, in particular the often advanced view that hooks should break clear of baits on the strike. It also contradicts those anglers who believe that hooks are detectable, and that shy pike will reject a bait if they feel a big hook. On the face of it, nothing is more detectable than a size 2 lashed at 90° to the bait.

An article that Barrie Rickards wrote for *Coarse Angler* provoked a glimmer of understanding. He discussed the way a pike dealt with its prey, based on his observations. He saw a pike pick up a bait crosswise in its jaws. The bait was then manoeuvred to a position from which it could be swallowed *without the jaws of the pike actually moving*. Barrie could only assume that it was using its tongue. He then suggested that a bait would not be manipulated as quickly or as easily in this way if there were hooks on the flank, and for that reason he favoured small rather than big trebles. With our rig there are no hooks of any size in the flank. The bait can be taken to the swallowing position without the pike feeling anything, and once in that position a bait is inhaled in a flash.

The bigger pike possibly engulf the whole bait in one go, but I have never seen a very big pike take a deadbait. What I can confidently assert is that they must invariably deal with a deadbait before we detect a run or in the very early stages of that run. If they did not we would not have had a near 100 per cent hooking record in the last two seasons.

How transferable this rig might be is for you to discover, but it has had one failure away from the pits. I fished a couple of Barrie's drain fisheries at the end of the 1990–1 season. Conditions were far from perfect and the fish were finicky. They seemed to be picking the bait up and simply swimming around with it. I have encountered that at odd times in the past, but not on the pit.

In those circumstances a hook in the flank is going to be the only method likely to succeed on an early strike. I missed my only run on the first day, and two or three the following day as well. Barrie reckoned that I was striking too quickly, which is probably true. Behaviour can vary from water to water; his pike obviously take longer than mine to deal with a bait.

You must always be prepared for differences, including differences between your gravel pits and mine, of course, but I will be surprised if the versatile approach is not the best for all of them.

6

BOAT FISHING FOR PIKE

The most important rule to follow when you set off boat fishing for pike is to wear a life-jacket – this is common sense. Today's life-jackets are activated by compressed CO_2 which are designed to lift your head and shoulders above the water in the event of an accident. You will find that the jacket fits neatly under your fishing coat.

The second most important rule is that you should never set out in a boat if the troughs between the waves would encompass the average family saloon. Such conditions are not piking weather. But a good wave is beneficial to piking afloat as it is often to bank fishing, so it is not necessary to wait for a glassy calm.

There are several items a boat angler needs which rarely come with the boat. One is an anchor rope of about 100ft. The rope should be soft enough and thick enough to grip and pull on, even if you are wearing gloves. Avoid some of the hard nylons as they are very prone to kinks and nasty knots and they remove your skin in seconds. You need mud anchors and 'real' anchors. For the latter, ask the advice of a ship's chandler according to the size of boat you have or will be using. Anchors are not very expensive, even those with break-away facilities. Mud anchors are simply the appropriate weight of concrete in a plastic bucket and fitted with a ring. All anchors benefit from having a length of chain attached to the rope, so that the chain lies on the bottom and helps purchase. It is a good idea to have a bows and stern anchor facility and, in the bows at least, a roller or bearer over which to haul the rope.

If your oars work in rowlocks, you will need a safety attachment to keep both of them attached to the gunwales. There is nothing worse when you are afloat then watching your dropped oar floating away downstream. The Irish thole pins seem to be superior to rowlocks, because anglers do not require fine tuning of the rowing, but reliability of the single thrust and release. (However, avoid those rare English compromises where, instead of a thole pin block on the oar, you see a hole drilled *through* the oar.)

Outboard motors seem to be reliable nowadays and decent-sized engines more affordable; however, I would always have an electric outboard motor as a back-up and a trolling facility if possible.

Boat fishing often begins and ends in the dark in winter and good teamwork is essential. Here Colin Brett, Tim Cole and John Milford return after a day's piking several miles from base

No regular boat-going piker should be without a graph echo-sounder. Those which give you a visible graph recorder screen and print-out if needed are invaluable. It is important to remember that the transducer on the echo-sounder is delicate and should be protected from damage, especially when it is at risk during landing. Mine is set into a plastic tube which hangs neatly over the gunwales. On landing I either swing up the plastic tube by hand or, if the shore is sandy or grassy, I allow the beaching of the boat to do it for me. The display section of the echo-sounder I usually have in a cardboard box surrounded by bubble plastic foam, just for protection to keep it clean. Should it rain, a section of the bubble plastic pulls forward and hangs down like curtain over the screen itself. It is also worth remembering that if your echo-sounder shows dangerous rocks looming up, it is too late to take avoiding action because they are under the boat. Always use an echo-sounder in conjunction with charts and maps, and don't just concentrate on the screen and the rod tip.

Although I have often thought that we take noise too seriously in pike fishing, there is no question that a clattered oar or tackle box will disturb pike.

There are several ways of avoiding unnecessary noise. One way is to clad the bottom boards in a sheet of bubble plastic, or old carpet or sacking. This does deaden the noise, and has the added advantage that when you are dealing with a pike inboard there is a protective substrate to put it on. You can also press on to the gunwales (lightly Copydexed) piping insulation foam. This means that you can lay a rod across the thwarts without worrying about whether the line is being abraded; this can be done quickly and quietly.

Personal comfort is important while you are piking afloat, and you need both good foams to sit on, and a bucket as a baler or to pee into. Never urinate over the side of the boat in rough weather; or for females, not at all, because the centre of gravity (if not buoyancy) shifts alarmingly and there is the danger of falling overboard.

Be shipshape and try to get a routine worked out with whoever you happen to be sharing a boat with. Teamwork is vital and takes a great deal of hard work and worry out of the exercise. Tell your partner what you are doing and why. One person may ship the oars, while the other mans the anchor rope, etc. Tim Cole and I load up Colin Brett's 17ft boat in about three minutes from unloading the car to firing the outboard; everything is secured in its regular place, preferably under the seats or in lockers, and we each know what the other has done with a piece of gear. Similar attitudes are necessary for landing, beaching on a shore, fixing position to fish, and so on. When the boating also involves a camping expedition to some remote vantage point, such efficiency makes for greater enjoyment of the trip, and it allows room for laughs rather than lamentation.

The tackle needs some modification, but not a great deal, for boat fishing. I tend to use stronger lines from a boat, because the line is always more at risk of physical abrasion on the boat parts than on the general softness of a river bank. Many anglers prefer to use multiplier reels when they are boat fishing, but the bait-runner facility now available on fixed spool reels reduces the advantage of multipliers of paying off line to an audible tick, in the event of a run. What *are* undeniably valuable to the boat enthusiast are boat-rod rests. These hold the butt of the rod over the gunwales and the rod as a whole over the side, so that the inboard area remains uncluttered. You can buy them from such firms as Trevor Moss of Gainsborough, or you can inspect the commercial product and make your own by welding up ¼in black mild steel. You then wrap them in insulating tape to be kind to the rod and its cosmetics. Tie the rod rests with cord to the boat, otherwise, if the G-clamp slips, you could lose a valuable item in a way that could mar the trip.

Lures can be kept in cantilever boxes on boats, and you can hang a piece of old carpet over the gunwales in which to impale those lures that are in most constant use. Carpet grips the hooks so that they do not become tangled up or dropped on the deck where they will be trodden on.

One hears some romantic tales of battling pike from boat anglers. Of course, the stories are true but some of the reasoning is suspect. One hears, for example praise of the immense power of a pike as it tows the boat all over the loch/lough. If you are using a line of, say, 12lb breaking strain, then the pull of the pike at no time exceeds 12lb. If it did, the line would break. You can test this easily enough for yourself. Stand in the shallows at the prow of your craft and attach the hook of a balance to the bow, and then pull the boat through the water, reading the balance as you go. You will discover that a 16ft clinker-built Shannon longboat will respond smoothly to a pull of only a few pounds. I was once pulled all over Killinure Lough by a fish of 6lb. When playing pike from a boat it is helpful if a partner drops the anchor. If you do not, the fight can last for some time, which could be deleterious to the health of the fish.

Always use the biggest boat you can obtain for boat fishing. Small boats are only useful for the individual and are not helpful on big waters. I last used my 10ft dinghy extensively on Ardingley Reservoir, and Colin Simpson, who ran the place in those days and is an experienced sailor and mariner, was always enthusiastic about the organisation and shipshapeness of my little craft. But

It is better to sit down in a boat as the fish nears the craft before netting (or, in this case, hand-gaffing)

one should not get carried away with one's enthusiasm: Ardingley is the biggest water a 10ft dinghy should be afloat on.

Approach work to a swim where you intend to anchor up and fish is something which only experience can teach you. Almost always the beginner overshoots his site and has to come in again, adding to the disturbance. Ideally, one should come in downwind, thus avoiding traversing the area to be fished, and drop at least one anchor early. You can then judge the effect of drift and wind on the boat before you move quietly a little closer. This last move can be made by just lifting the anchor clear of the bottom, even allowing it to drag slightly, and letting the drift move you into position. Drop the anchor a fraction short of where you want to be to allow for the purchase to take hold. As the water gets deep, say, in excess of 20ft this kind of approach is critical. By the time you actually anchor you will know how much rope is needed under the prevailing conditions. If all this can be achieved on one anchor, the moment you add the effect of a second, you will be even more stable.

Not much can prevent the boat from swinging and drifting, especially over deep water, so set up your rigs to allow for this. Multipliers, bait-runners, or ordinary fixed-spool reels with the slipping clutch set almost to zero, are the order for the day. After a while, a fixed amount of slack line is created, and this is taken up alternatively or released as the boat swings. Use floats if possible, and concentrate carefully, otherwise bites will be too well developed by the time you spot them, and you may mistake a run for wind drift. Centrepin reels can also be used efficiently and comfortably from a boat.

Avoid using a landing net with a long handle because it often gets in the way. A big net will work well with a handle about 1ft or so long. Having netted a fish, either hold the net in the water by hand, or hang it on a rowlock, while you get things tidied inboard and an area ready to receive the pike; the forceps, net and camera should also be ready, of course. Again, orderliness helps, as does a modicum of planning. It is common sense to use the minimum of rods while you are afloat, but anglers refuse to follow this advice because they are tempted into using an excessive number of rods because of the available 360° turning area. The same anglers are probably unaware that a fast-travelling pike can tangle up the lines in ten seconds – but they will only learn from experience.

The great advantage of boat fishing is that it gives you access to swims that are impossible to reach from the bank even by drift fishing, and it also enables you to reach bank swims that might otherwise be difficult to reach. But boat fishing also requires the traditional bank pike angler to consider safety, organisation and piking technique. Approached soberly and sensibly, boat fishing is a worthwhile experience that can be highly productive.

THE DUTCH EXPERIENCE

Colin Dyson

It has been my privilege to meet a number of the great pike anglers – Bill Giles, Reg Sandys, Dennis Pye and Frank Wright in the old days; Barrie Rickards and Nev Fickling in more recent years. The Dutchman Bert Rozemeijer is in the same class, and possibly more successful in terms of big fish caught than anyone mentioned here. We will never know for sure, simply because in the great heyday of Dutch pike fishing Bert and his fellow countrymen were interested in the lengths of pike, not their weights. They still speak of 'X-centimetre pike' or 'metre pike', which are almost certainly twenty-pounders in Holland. Bert, however, has never even bothered to record his metre pike, and did not catch the habit of weighing his fish until recently, when he was corrupted by contacts with Englishmen like me.

I have seen Bert catch a thirty-five-pounder, which was weighed and returned with total nonchalance. It was not a personal best, he told me, but he did not say what his best was, or how many thirty-pounders he had landed. Some time later, I put on the front page of *Coarse Angler* the monstrous fish which registered 43lb while it was still not quite clear of the ground. When it did clear it, the fish smashed Bert's weighing equipment. We would have done anything to get that pike weighed properly, but Bert just put it back. The welfare of the fish mattered to him far more than its weight.

It is useless asking someone like Bert what they have caught, because I don't think he either knows or cares. He once let slip that he probably caught about twenty fish over 20lb in most seasons, but numbers and figures are irrelevant to him. Bert just loves pike of any size; he is like a schoolboy when he is catching tiddler pike on the fly in what he calls the Peat Bog Lakes, an area of Holland which is remarkably like the Norfolk Broads.

It was Bert's fortune to be fishing the great lakes of Holland when they were at their peak. Some of the better-known lakes are past their best now, and we visiting Englishmen have found them very difficult. Other and still productive waters are not so well known, and Bert reveals them to us only a little at a time.

The last time I was in Holland we fished a huge lake, but there were only two other anglers on it. Bert and his friends had taken a lot of big fish there in the summer, but in early winter it was tough. We 'found' big pike on the graph recorder – great shapes which made us wonder what on earth they must weigh. Bert reckoned the lake was good for at least one 40lb pike in a year, but for us it gave up but one little jack.

. That is the sort of environment Bert has operated in for many years, and he has studied his quarry in tremendous detail. The advent of graph recorders allowed him to build on what he had previously learned the hard way. He

Colin Dyson with a 30lb fish from one of the large, deep, Dutch waters – the capture a direct result of the techniques outlined in this chapter

noted, for example, that on these big and often very deep waters resting pike – which is what you mostly locate on the graph – simply suspended on the thermocline between meals.

The thermocline is the area where the warmer upper layers of water meet that which is permanently the same temperautre. The depth at which that happens varies with the seasons – it is deeper in summer and much closer to the surface in winter. Since the prey shoals were usually above the thermocline, Bert knew that those resting pike were likely to go upwards to feed. Soon he knew the approximate depths at which to troll his baits at any given time of year, fine-tuning his approach on a day-to-day basis.

If you go out on a big lake like Het Twiske, near Amsterdam, at dawn, you will see evidence to back Bert's findings. Large shoals of fish, roach and bream in the main, will be priming on the surface. Occasionally, you will see a great swirl as a sizeable fish becomes breakfast for some leviathan – taken off the top in maybe 100ft of water. Imagine the pike going back down with, say, a 3–4lb bream inside it. The pike is back on that layer of cold water, its metabolism slowing down. Think how long such a meal will last that fish. Think of the remarkably short time in which that pike is vulnerable to a bait presented by an angler. It will be resting again for many days, until the stirrings of hunger propel it upwards once again. So vast is the prey fish population that the pike can be back on the thermocline just a few minutes later, for another long stay. What are the odds against it finding your bait, even if you are lucky enough to be passing at exactly the right time? Obviously, they are not very great, but fortunately there are many pike in a great range of sizes. When a lot of pike are vulnerable, if only for a few minutes each, the cause of the intelligent angler is far from lost.

If you fish in the right way in the right place, your jackpot will eventually fall, as mine did in Holland in 1990. A 30lb fish engulfed a perch livebait pushing 1lb in weight. Several minutes of violent, elemental battle, pulses racing, heart pounding, then silent prayers and euphoria – this is what the days and weeks of patient trolling are supposed to achieve. You plan it, dream about it. You know, deep down, that it will happen one day, for that is both the faith and the instinct of a committed angler. If you don't believe that it will happen, it very likely won't.

I am happiest as a pike angler when my imagination can run free, and it runs riot in Holland. There is so much water and those huge marks on the graph to enjoy; and Bert Rozemeijer's air of calm authority, which you know will lead from one triumph to another, is an inspiration. All you don't know is how much time will elapse in between, and whether you will be successful on that trip, the next or the one after that.

For me, the sheer bliss of being in Holland outweighs the dream of success. I know that I might catch a couple of twenty-pounders and a few doubles if I spent the time at home, but I have happily traded that for half a chance of one great fish. The thirty-pounder was a stepping-stone; it was not the fish which fires the imagination, for that is always bigger than one's best. It sounds like greedy ambition, but it is not. It is just a dream which might become reality if I work at it hard enough. It is a dream which keeps me going through the long and fishless days, although I have not been bored for a single moment while trolling.

To be honest, I have caught fewer fish trolling than by any other method. Efficient trolling on big waters depends on the accurate presentation of a bait at a chosen depth, usually along some feature like the near bank drop-off. Having done it blind on waters of irregular depth I have no wish to do so again, not when a graph recorder can stop me blundering into shallows, pinnacles of rock and snags which can claim my baited hooks, which might then become a death-trap for a pike.

Barrie mentions in Chapter 6 that when your graph tells you that you are in rocky shallows it is too late to take avoiding action, but it is not always so. It can be a problem on waters where pinnacles of rock thrust their way suddenly towards the surface in otherwise deep water, which is the case in both Scotland and Ireland. Most waters are more predictable, however, and when using a graph it is easy to change direction when you see that you are losing depth. The baits are 10–20yd behind, sometimes more, and gentle manipulation of either the oars or an electric motor will keep them operating in the chosen depth.

After fishing with Bert Rozemeijer for a while I soon discovered that he was using the graph more for confirmation of depth than for information. He now knows his waters very well. Indeed, one large water I have fished often is mapped in my own mind. It would not matter much to me now if I fished it blind, but I would miss the absolute precision which the graph grafts on to the technique. Knowing that you are doing exactly what you want to do is a great confidence-booster. I would also miss the additional information provided by graphs, which are becoming ever more sophisticated. Basically, they all rely on sound waves which bouce back off the bottom and anything intervening – usually fish and shoals of fish. The information is recorded either on a paper read-out or on a liquid crystal display.

The paper read-out is excellent for mapping waters, for you are left with a permanent record of any journey between chosen landmarks – exact depths, all the changes on contour, even the nature of the bottom, whether it is hard or soft. Provided the journey is done at a constant speed, and the paper is marked at the beginning and at the end of the run, you have an absolutely accurate picture. Make parallel runs from north to south for example, and then do the same from east to west, and the depths will hold no more secrets. Plumbing to achieve the same results is almost impossible.

Unfortunately, graph paper is very expensive, and the LCD graphs are vastly more preferable for actual trolling work. It brings a totally new dimension to your fishing. I think I learned more about big lakes in a few weeks than I had in the previous two decades, and not just about the depths and contours. I learned mostly about the fish themselves – for example, how they mass in certain areas, leaving vast tracts of water apparently empty. I never realised how much time the shoals spend in the top half of the water.

It is remarkable how the tiniest features – for example, a small bump on the bottom – attract fish. And after a while the marks they make on screen betray the species which is making them. In the Dutch environment a little bump on the bottom seems to be a preferred area for zander or small pike which, Bert has established, choose to live with the zander in the deeps. If they wander to the top of the water before they are big enough, they are too vulnerable to the bigger pike.

Watching prey fish shoals scrolling by on the screen heightens anticipation. If there are any hungry predators they are not going to be far away, although at times the sheer numbers of prey fish diminish the confidence that one's bait could possibly be selected. One day on Het Twiske a vast shoal of bream literally blacked out the screen for a distance of about 200yd. They seemed to be at every level in quite a depth of water. When you see that, you realise how simple it is for the big pike to find an easy meal.

In the main you find shoals which are less numerous and more scattered, and the depth at which they are mostly swimming is one of the clues which point to the depth at which to set a trolled live- or deadbait, or a lure. Bert prefers plugs and spoons in the warmer months, trolled at a speed rather faster than a live- or deadbait. He has shown me big Rapala plugs which have been chewed literally to pieces, exposing their internal wirework. It is clearly a hectic game at times, but I have not yet had the pleasure of sharing one of those days with him.

All my trips have had to be in late autumn or winter, when Bert has switched to live- and deadbait trolling. He has always known the depths at which pike are suspending, whatever the time of the year, and the approximate depths at which he is likely to catch them. On most of my trips we have fished the 5–8yd contours, with the baits set to fish at about half those depths. If two or three baits are being fished, one might be 1yd higher, another 1yd lower. The aim is to cover as much water as possible, vertically and horizontally, but before I explain that in more detail it is perhaps the right moment to discuss the tackle and the trolling rig.

Berts favours a 13ft rod, and his is made of glass. It has a beautiful action when he plays a fish, and it is the right length for proper control. I appreciated what he meant by that when I hooked my big fish, for, after towing the boat sideways for some distance, it suddenly turned and ran straight back towards the boat. It went right under the middle of the boat, where I was standing, and I had to pass the rod round one end in order to follow it. That was relatively easy with a 13ft rod (a 3lb TC rod made for me by Pete Evans); it might have been a different story with a well-bent 11-footer.

Barrie Rickards has observed elsewhere in this book how easy it is to propel a boat on water, and I have made the same point myself several times over the years. Bert's boat is a big one, however, and was loaded with three people and their tackle. Towing it sideways, especially against a wind, imposes some degree of strain on the tackle, requiring rapid mental adjustments on how to play a big fish safely.

We knew that it was a very big fish because it had surfaced almost under the rod at a very early stage in the battle. I normally play pike off the handle, but where very big pike are possible I also set the clutch; I do this fairly tightly, but at a setting which should give line before it breaks. For a brief moment I thought that I could hold that pike and let it tow itself to a standstill, but I changed my mind when the boat gathered pace, the rod bent further than I had ever seen it go and the clutch began a reluctant and ominous protest. I played safe, backwinding throughout an initial run of about 50yd, and again after the pike had gone under the boat for another run of 50yd. I was on the wrong side of safety with a 12lb line in which I have every confidence at home. I would not go again without Terry Eustace's Big Game line, the '12lb' which breaks at 16lb plus. I achieved less than three-quarters of what is possible in Holland; a much bigger fish might have caught me out.

With regard to reels, multipliers have a lot of advantages for trolling, but I am not keen on them. I don't think I would have kept in touch with my fish with a multiplier when it turned and ran back at me. Multipliers have no real advantages over modern fixed spools like the Shimano Baitrunner 4000/4500s. They hold hundreds of yards of strong line, and the bait-runner facility is great for trolling. You just set it so that it only just won't give line on the troll, but a striking fish can take line without any resistance.

The right type of floats for trolling were a problem for all anglers, including the Dutch, but it was the Dutch who solved the problem. Because of the depths at which the baits are often set to run the floats have to be sliders, running to a bead and a Power Gum stop-knot. Unfortunately, sliding floats tend to push down the line against the water pressure, thus lifting the baits above the chosen depth.

When I first went to Holland, the Dutch were using self-locking floats with a curved hole running from the bottom and out at the side. They were difficult to make, but effective. A year or so later, however, Dutch anglers were attaching them to a simple but clever device, a curved piece of tubing with a swivel coming off the middle. The line runs through the tubing until the tubing hits the stop-knot, then locks in place under tension.

Immediately I saw the possibilities for float-ledgering at home, as well as trolling, and wrote a piece about it for *Coarse Angler*. Use the float-ledger with long floats, which come to the top and lie flat when the bait hits the bottom. Tighten until the float cocks, and you have bite registration second to none. The float falls flat the second a pike picks up the bait.

You can make a perfectly serviceable lock by putting a piece of thickish copper wire through a length of Biro tubing and bending it to the right shape. Pour boiling water over it and plunge immediately into cold water. Finally, pull the wire out.

The best floats for trolling are the rotund bungs which we used to scorn on the old livebaiting rigs. I did my share of that myself, believing that such floats offered far too much resistance. Now I think we were wrong. Those floats were the original bolt rigs, but we didn't know it. We still don't accept them, even though we know pike will happily run off with a bait and 2–3oz of fixed lead.

Resistance/weight is acceptable as long as it is felt immediately. However, if you let a pike run free and then offer it a tiny bit of resistance, it may well drop the bait. I once had a string of dropped runs before discovering the cause – a forgotten stop-knot, which was snatching for a brief moment as it ran through the bomb.

Trolling floats need to be substantial enough to support a large bait and a lead of a sufficient size to hold the bait most of the time at the chosen depth. If a livebait can pull the float down for a while at the start, and at odd intervals after that, it is about right. Downriggers are perhaps more efficient at present-ing a bait at an exact depth, but I much prefer the float. Watching it keeling over as the bait swims up a bit keeps you in touch with what is happening. It is often the prelude to a run. Such anticipation and excitement is denied to those who use downriggers.

At the business end of the tackle is a drilled bullet of about $^1/_2$oz and I like to take a rubber or plastic sleeve through it to protect the line from chafing. The trace wire needs to be strong, and Bert has such respect for the power of his quarry that he makes a new trace after every good fish. He uses plastic-covered wire, which we rejected many moons ago because the wire and cover-ing stretch at different rates, causing awful wrinkling. There is no problem if you use a strong plastic-covered wire, but if it is changed after every good fish it doesn't matter.

Bert likes plastic-covered wire because his crimps bite into it, making a slip impossible, and he seems to own the only crimping tool in the world which produces the same neat result that we see on some commercially made traces. He bought it years ago in Holland, but they are no longer available.

Vic Bellars usually makes the traces for the Dutch market, using 28lb wire, crimps and Araldite. They are as foolproof as we can make them, and they are armed with big trebles. It is pointless hunting big pike on the troll with small baits. Good-sized herrings and mackerel are the order of the day, or livebaits of 10oz plus. Bert generally uses size 2 or 4 Partridge outpoint trebles. For our traces Vic used formidable MP trebles, which are very strong in the wire.

The rigs have a large single which goes through the lips of the baits, and two trebles. Bert insists, and I believe he is right, that one of the trebles must go very close to the head, no further back than the pectorals. He believes that pike target the head, and those who have done some lure fishing will agree. If there is a hook at the front end of a lure, as there is on a Kuusamo Professor spoon, for example, it is surprising how often that hook, and not the seemingly more obvious tail end hook, catches the pike.

The second hook goes in the flank of the bait, just beyond half-way, and on the same side as the other hook. That is very important, for we are now back to the point where I broke off to consider the tackle.

On the day that I caught my thirty-pounder Bert suddenly noticed that I had my hooks in the wrong side of the bait. Bert has a very dry sense of humour, and at first I thought that he was joking. But no, he was serious. My bait was operating nearest the drop-off – the favourite position. His was immediately behind the boat, with Vic Bellars' bait on the other side. My float and Bert's were operating close together, because his bait was armed down the left side and mine were down the right flank, the water pressure on the hooks was pushing the baits together. When I switched my hooks to the left side my bait immediately swung out closer to the drop-off. It made several yards of difference.

Now the tackle is right and the trolling contour has been chosen. From this point it is a waiting game – a slow and steady amble around the contour. The graph tells the oarsman or motorman when to change direction to keep on the contour. Sometimes a little extra speed and a change of direction is tried for no reason, except that it manipulates the baits and causes the floats to skate and accelerate – rather like sink-tip fly fishing from a drifting boat, when the takes usually come as the fly is accelerating around the curve. It is not an obvious manoeuvre; the changes are so subtle that it was a while before I realised that Bert was doing it deliberately.

It was such a manoeuvre that caught Bert's 35-pounder. The boat moved to port. Bert's float, working the drop-off on the starboard side, was the first to register the direction change. It picked up pace while mine, momentarily, stood still. The floats, several yards apart a few moments earlier, were now almost together. And then there was but one above the surface – mine. Two years and many trolling miles later it was to be the other way around. These are rare, moments, Magic moments. . . well worth waiting for.

7

CRACKING A NEW WATER

PREPARATION

One of the great pleasures in piking, if not *the* pleasure, is in going where other anglers have *not* been, or but rarely. I will not be discussing discovering a water through the usual channels. If you ask in a tackle shop, then any water recommended to you will already have some kind of a name for pike, and the same applies if you follow the press reports. First, try to find out which waters produce really good match fishing bags on a regular basis, but rarely, if ever, mention pike attacking the keep-nets. If the latter is happening, then you are much too late, because the better pike will have been caught one or two seasons before and the match anglers will now be reaping the benefit – lots of small pike. Of course, if that's what you want . . .

Often it is possible to find a productive water – for example, for roach and bream which, you will be told, 'has no pike in it'. These can be absolute winners for pike fishing because it means that the pike have not been fished for, or even their presence recognised, and there are certain to be relatively small numbers of pike, of quite big fish. It is crucial to keep quiet about your catches and to fish at times when other anglers are not there.

Next, you need to get an Ordnance Survey 1:50,000 map and scour it for waters. Armed with the map I drive around the countryside, inspecting in real life what were blue marks on the map. I chat to anglers on the bank and talk to bailiffs. This kind of work is best done in the close season, because although there will be no anglers on the bank, you will find that the club official has more time to stop and talk.

After you have found a water that seems promising, you need to draw a plan or sketch map of the place and either go there with the boat and echo-sounder, or plumb the depth manually, from the bank. In any event, you will need to know the contours of the water and all its physical features. Carefully note due north. This will be vital when you consider wind directions. You will need to know exactly what effect a south-westerly blow has on the water, because it is usually from the south-west that the big blows come. Does it

Author with a big fish which fell to half sardine deadbait on a small water

Barrie Rickards gently returning a big pike

make some swims unfishable? Does it give access, by drifter rigs, to some part you could not normally reach? Where will the cold/warm water go when various winds blow? Where will the undertows be? All these things can be worked out in a matter of minutes once you know where north is. However, it is well to observe the effects of wind directly, because banks, woodland, hills or buildings can often deflect or channel wind into unexpected directions at water level, and that is where its effect counts. On one drain that Tim Cole and I used to fish, a southerly breeze used to end up as a force 4–5 westerly.

When a lake is big, some of these observations may be both time-consuming and difficult, especially if you have no boat or are not allowed a boat. First, try to find out if there are any aerial photographs, such as in the local council office. Such photographs often show very clearly gravel bars and shallows, as well as weed-beds.

Satellite pictures are also available nowadays. Some of these are remarkably detailed, but they are of more use on the very big waters like Loch Lomond. Also for the big waters you can often get Admiralty Charts, and, with their precise depths and bottom conditions, they are invaluable to boat anglers. I have used these charts on a number of waters in my early forays, and still take them with me even when I know the water well. Finally, those big gravel pits are probably in plan form in the local council offices.

In summary, use every means initially to find a new venue and secondly to understand its physical character. You will then have you own chart or sketch map, annotated with all you have managed to find out.

Occasionally, however, it may not be necessary to do this immediately. A simple stroll around or along the water may inspire you to have a dabble. After that, I suggest you try spinning. This has some disadvantages, because if the pike are on a bait-taking exercise, you may go straight past a hotspot and not know it. But often it does produce a fish or two and the location of the takes may usefully identify an area worth trying, more slowly, with baits. Apart from anything else it is a good way to see your first few fish from a water, and it enables you to cover a considerable extent of the bank. Furthermore, spinning helps you to get a quick idea of depths and the snags like sunken trees. However, if you use a spinnerbait or buzzer, with a single, inturned hook, you are unlikely to snag up (except on fish), yet you will feel the snags as you bounce through them. Underwater weed-beds can also be found, as can rapid breaks in slope and similar features. You need to know the rate of sink of a particular lure – for example, a $1/2$oz buzzer sinks at 1ft per second.

For the angler who has just had five runs in his winter season and is keen on a successful new season, a short-cut to success on a new water, which I emphasise will result in success with pike, though not necessarily big pike is as follows. He should drive around his county in June and July and look for a

Tim Cole with a big twenty-pounder from a fenland drain only 16 feet wide and 2 feet deep

shallow gravel pit complex or shallow drain or river system – say, 3–5ft deep – which is absolutely choked with weeds. The chances are that such a water will not be fished during the summer and autumn, except perhaps by tench anglers who rake swims. The same waters will not be fished by pike anglers in winter unless they are 'named' waters (when 5–10 runs per winter are the norm), partly because they saw them in the summer. Yet such waters often teem with pike because they are so productive. If the weed is blanket weed – algae caused by excess nutrient supplies – then he should wait until October or November when most of it will have died back. If, however, the weed is water-lily or pond weeds of various kinds, he should fish a spinnerbait or buzzer through it, or a plastic spoon on the top of it. I can guarantee that you will catch plenty of pike using this method.

Your initial impression may be that the pike are small, and certainly you will get plenty in the 1–5lb bracket, especially in the weed in summer. But if the water is more than a few acres, it will almost certainly have a few big fish too – remember, we are talking about a relatively unfished water because of the sight that puts off most anglers, namely thick weeds. You next need to try to work out where any better pike might be: in a deeper than normal hole, per- haps; in an inaccessible corner, or beneath overhanging willows, and so on. At this stage you will need as much data as you can. By this stage, however, you will have already exceeded in catches the total number of runs you had last year, and your time will be due for a good, memorable fish.

The chances of finding a hotspot on a first visit to a water are rather remote. There may be nothing at all to give them away save a tight concentration of bigger pike. Miss that concentration by 20yd and you might just as well be a mile away. On the other hand, you do need to give a water a good try. While it is ill-advisable to start fishing before daybreak, it certainly is a good idea to begin as early as possible. If it is to be a one-run day, then the chances are that that run will occur earlier rather than later.

A CAMBRIDGE GRAVEL PIT

One of the gravel pit complexes that I got to know well was just north of Cambridge, near Waterbeach. They varied somewhat but were generally weedy. A walk around the water wasn't too appealing, partly because it was heavily fished by bottom fishermen and partly because of thick weed-growth. As I reached the far side of the lake, several hundred yards from the road, I noticed a clump of trees across a meadow that looked as though they might be growing around a pond. A few minutes later I found a kidney-shaped lake, which was equally choked with weed and about 3 acres in size. I could find only one spot that someone had tried to fish, and one bank was almost inaccessible with heavy willow growth, fallen trees and brambles. The water was crystal clear and I could see shoals of fry among the weeds.

Although I was not too optimistic, I fetched my spinning rod and began by working a Crazy Crawler across the top of the weeds, which were thick enough to weed it up for part of each cast. Then it was taken by a slashing strike and I reeled in a very plump perch of about 1/2lb. They seemed suckers for the surface lure on this water and I caught a few of them, all from an area in the middle of the water, and the taking spot was perhaps 50yd from the inaccessible bank. The perch were all very solid fish, but none was over a pound or so. Nevertheless, there was quite a shoal of them, and as I fished I got the feeling that the weed was a bit clearer in that area; possibly the water was a little deeper.

After examining the rest of the pit carefully and getting a jack pike of 1/2lb on a spoon, I decided that two swims, one each side of the lake, would give me the possibility of throwing a deadbait up into the spot were the perch were feeding. The positions of sunken trees had to be allowed for; if there was a decent fish there at all I wanted to give myself a chance of pulling it away from snags and not into them.

That first visit to the water was in September 1971, and I eventually arrived with baits on 9 November of that year fully expecting the weed to have died down – it hadn't. Even so, my 'spot' was identifiable and I set up the Oliver's 10ft glass rod and a solidly frozen half mackerel just at first light. The cast over-shot the mark by about 5yd, so I held the rod high and skittered the bait back across the surface, dropping it into exactly the right place. A commotion broke out in the little lake and ripples spread to the other end. I had used a float because I didn't want the line to sink into soft weed between me and the bait, but the float lay on its side, clearly indicating that my 8ft depth was a little opti-mistic. I tightened up gently and then dropped an empty reel spool over the line below the reel, and weighted it down slightly with gravel. The second rod, also with a half mackerel on it, I cast in a high arc down the lake so that it came down vertically, like a bomb, and went straight through the surface weeds.

At 8.30 the plastic spool on the first rod suddenly catapulted for yards, and line zipped off the spool at a sprint. There was no let up, so I put in the pick-up and waited. A second later the rod tip whipped round. I had it up high and there was a servere curve in the glass. Then a tremendous explosion occured beneath one of the weed-beds. The line entered the weeds in one place and the boil was 10yd away at an angle to the left. I heaved and pulled to try to get the line straight to the fish. It was certainly well on. By keeping the rod up high I managed to get a fair bit of line out of the water, but plenty of weed was hang-ing on it at water level, putting a lot of strain on the whole outfit. Suddenly the pike made a terrific surge in the other direction, travelling just beneath the surface, and at last the line straightened out, showering cut weed in all

The author returning a big gravel-pit pike

directions. The fish was now free of encumbrances but for some reason it didn't dive, and a few minutes later I was able to haul it, still thrashing spray, over the waiting net. It weighed 21lb exactly, a superbly conditioned fish. A week later, in exactly the same spot, to the same technique I got a shorter, fatter fish of 20½lb. Later there were a few doubles, and in the following January I had the 21lb fish again, this time well after dark on a small livebait. Over several seasons that water gave great pleasure, both with pike and perch. It was not, of course, the sort of water that one would flog week after week, but to have in one's repertoire such a water close to hand was satisfying. It was four years before I saw another angler on the water.

A NORFOLK DRAIN

As a second example let me take a tiny, unfished drain in Norfolk. I had looked at it several times, after seeing a thin blue line on an Ordnance Survey map. It was way off the beaten track, rather desolate in outlook, but with a great deal of wildlife, including kingfishers, harriers and herons. The water itself was shallow and coloured, but in the winter when I examined it, it was almost weed free.

The first spot I chose because the access was reasonably good, down a cart track. I arrived a couple of hours before dark on the last day in October, and there had been a wintry look about the weather all that month. This evening was the same: clear, cold and with high, scudding clouds. I cast two half herring baits, one upstream from where I sat and one downstream, and I sat back to enjoy the solitude. About half an hour later the upstream float simply set off further upstream. There was no bob, no fuss, it simply submerged as it went, and kept going. I hit the run immediately and was rewarded with a tigerish battle before a fish of 11¼lb hit the net.

The next morning I was back again, in position at dawn, and at 9.30 I had caught a 7¼lb pike on small livebait; fifteen minutes later I had one of 8½lb on the same bait; and at 10.15 I had one of 14lb again on a small livebait. In the meantime, I had pulled out of a fish on a plug, of about 9lb or so, but the deadbait had not moved. I was just sitting back very smugly, when the water started to run like a salmon river, and quickly ran down to about 1½ft deep of brown water. I reeled in the gear and decided to sit this one out. Surely they couldn't take much more out?

Nevertheless, I was confident enough here. It turned out to be misplaced confidence, because half an hour later the farmer turned up and turned me off his land. I had asked permission at the wrong farm. This farmer was very pleasant and polite, but did not want anglers on his land. He let me fish until lunchtime, but I did not get another run.

I made enquiries with other farmers in the area and over several years I caught a large number of double-figure fish and quite a few twenty-pounders up to 24lb. And they were caught in the most pleasant of conditions. An interesting feature of the water was that once I had found the hotspots, and fished them, they were still hotspots ten years later. And during those ten years I saw only one umbrella in the distance on one occasion and on another a couple of farmhands fishing for half an hour.

RIVER FISHERY

My third example is a river fishery in another county altogether. This particular water had a reputation in the early 1950s, but on the few occasions that I had been to look at it in the close season the banks seemed totally unfished. There was a lovely curve of the river in one section, so that the inside of the bend was like a point, and the river itself was rather wide. When I finally got around to visiting it one winter, it was clear that not an angler had been on the bank for months. It was all nicely grassed, with clumps of rush and weed along the edge.

As this particular section was somewhat isolated, and clearly not frequented, I began one morning just after dawn with three rods. It is, in fact, a good idea to fish a completely new water in daylight, otherwise you can find that you have cast your baits to the silliest of places. Each rod was on float-ledgered gear, and I intended to get the depths worked out by trial and error, which can be achieved fairly quickly with three deadbait rods out. Water depths seemed an even 12ft and the bottom was more or less clean and firm. Nothing happened all day. The date was 11 November and at about 3.45pm I had already packed away one rod into the holdall. Then the float on the middle rod disappeared and I could not tell whether drifting weed had caught the line or not. I tightened up gently, felt a thump, so hit it back. A few minutes later I netted a solid fish of 10$\frac{1}{2}$lb. The bait had been half a mackerel. That pike fought, and looked, as though it had never seen an angler, and for that reason alone I was prepared to have another go at the place.

I returned on 18 November under seemingly identical conditions with a south-westerly breeze. The actual fishing was easy, but a lead up to 1oz was needed to hold against the flow, and I found that I could dispense with the floats and at the same time get a better cast and avoid debris flowing down the river. Once again all seemed slow, until at 2.45pm my half mackerel tail again sailed away and I landed another good fish of 13$\frac{1}{2}$lb. Only fifteen minutes later the other indicator went (I was using only two rods) and after a terrific battle I landed a fish of 18$\frac{1}{4}$lb. It was in absolutely superb fettle, with not a mark on it, and very firmly built. At 3.45pm the same rod (with the same half

Wide, deep, slow rivers, such as the Great Ouse pictured here, almost always produce first-class pike fishing

mackerel bait) indicated again and this time a very heavy fish came straight towards me. I did not realise that it was hooked, and it simply swam into the net. It weighed 21½lb. On subsequent trips I took up to seven double-figure pike at a sitting, with the occasional twenty-pounder, and actually fished the water eight times before getting a fish under 10lb. During all that time, when I was fishing at weekends, I did not see another angler.

CLAY PIT

My next example concerns a clay pit, and it must be said immediately that these waters are among the most difficult to fish. It is my firm impression that the pike do not move about as much as fish in gravel pits, and finding the pockets of pike becomes a matter of prime importance.

As a young man I fished a particular clay pit in East Yorkshire for several years. In this case I had fished the water for bream and roach and was fairly familiar with it. However, it is surprising how ignorant the bottom fisherman can be of a water, for when Ray Webb and I began plumbing the depths, we found a system of channels over 10ft deep alongside the weed-beds. On examining a nearby clay pit, which was underway at the time, we could see why: the trucks ran along ridges while the clay was dug out between them. Such channel systems, which they become on flooding, are less regular by far than the ridge and hollow systems on gravel workings, and assumptions cannot be made about the whole water simply on a few depth determinations. We took the trouble to contour the whole lake, which took about three full days of work, casting with a heavy lead and sliding float.

Having determined where the gullies, flats and shallows were, as well as the sunken trees, we baited up several likely places and fished them with dead-baits. Our very first day produced results which I recall made Ray ecstatic for hours on end: fish of 9lb 4oz, 11lb and 9lb 14oz, which was remarkably good for those days. We went on to take many more good fish but no giants by modern standards. Eventually, we left it for pastures new. As confirmation that the pike did not move about much, we found that very delicate float rigs were needed for the bites. The pike did not run, but simply picked up the bait and swallowed it. We had, in fact, located the hotspots and pike are always prone to feed like this in their bailiwick. In clay pits the matter is exacerbated.

A different kind of water faced Tim Cole and myself in 1989 when we went as guests of Roy Westwood to a lake in Oxfordshire. Roy didn't know much about the water, except in terms of its carp, and the man running this stately home lake was unable to join us on the day. First we saw an island. To its left was a boat-house and weed-filled bay that looked tempting for lures; and to its right was a fair extent of open water that terminated in another bay with a small stream entering into it. Like the boat-house bay, there were plenty of lilies in evidence, although bankside access and casting would be tricky.

We opted for a plan of deadbaits into the deeper open waters for the first few hours of daylight, before we would think about exploring or fishing the weed-beds. There was boat too, so we could take the lure rods around the lake after lunch. All in all, we calculated that we ought to find fish if they were feeding at all.

The bottom turned out to be reasonably clean, with a little silkweed only, and the depth mostly upwards of 8ft but on a long cast nearer 12ft. We were optimistic on the static deadbaits, with two rods each in action. The optimism was misplaced, so by mid-morning I began spinning with buzzers. If the pike were not active in the open, deeper water, perhaps they were in the lily beds themselves. It is often the case, and so it proved on this occasion. Fishing into the lilies, using buzzers, is something very few anglers do, yet we have found it not only a good general technique, but one which so often gets you off to a start on a water. On this occasion we had fish to 14lb, and several nice pike.

After lunch we tried the boat and spun through several very promising sections, but only drew a blank. Only when the boat approached the boat-house and the extensive lily beds did we again contact fish, this time several small ones on giant Kilty spoons. In one day's fishing we had sorted out the whereabouts of a large number of pike, which would be an excellent starter if one were going on to fish it seriously. The total for the day was thirteen pike.

CANALS

One of the most difficult kinds of pike water to get to grips with are canals. These are one of the few types where I do concentrate on fishing features. On one Yorkshire canal I chose an area adjacent to a small side-stream. Close by was a lock and a turning bay with shallow water. It took me several miles of cycling to find anything out of the ordinary in this way, and when I did, the area was rather remote from the usual access points and impossible for cars to reach. On my first visit there I took both my bait gear as well as my spinning tackle, which was just as well. The dawn start resulted in no signs of interest, but fishing a plug through the swims gave a fish of 12lb. Other small fish followed, from the shallow turning bay, so I knew the area was resonably good. Subsequent trips not long after yielded pike of 10lb and 11lb and good sport in general both to baits and lures.

The reputation of the canal among the locals, I later discovered, was one of dourness with the occasional jacks turning up every few weeks. I had over twenty on the first four visits, so I felt well pleased, and kept quiet. As a general rule canals are difficult, even when good fish are known to be there. Obvious features are soon fished out if they are accessible, and the only alternative is to work along sections trip by trip, trying not to move too quickly. If there are two of you it is easier, especially if one of you is prepared to sit on the baits while the other lure fishes. Information from locals seems to pay off better on canals than on other waters, possibly because the habit of bottom fishermen of putting out a 'second rod' for pike dies hard on canals – they rarely have a current to contend with or other anglers too close for comfort. If the information you receive is more widely held than local, you are probably too late to find yourself a new venue. One final point about canals: if you locate pike near features, an active bait (lure- or livebait) seems best; when you locate them on long featureless sections, a static deadbait seems to work best. This may be a false impression on my part, but it is all that I have to go on for these most difficult of waters.

8

THE PRESENT AND THE FUTURE

Martin Gay

The art of fishing for pike is as old as angling itself, even though the emphasis has changed over the years from fishing for food to fishing for pleasure. Inversely, in proportion to this change in 'need' has been a vast improvement in our understanding of the species and the methods by which we now chase them. The greatest strides forward in this increased knowledge have been made in the last thirty years, although it is important to acknowledge the considerable input by such men as Bickerdyke, Norman Hill, among others, earlier this century and beyond. Perhaps because of the intervention of World War II, little happened between about 1930 and 1950, until around 1955 the Taylor 'brothers' (two brothers and one cousin) rediscovered the tactic of deadbaiting for pike.

Perhaps it was a coincidence that the Taylors brought this deadly technique of deadbaiting to our attention, at much the same time as angling in general was being 'rediscovered' and was receiving more attention in general terms once life began to settle after the war. It is important to note that any new technique, or method, or new water can only receive attention in any meaningful way if there are a number of 'progressive' anglers who are prepared to use and to develop the method and make known their findings.

Until recently pike angling had always been shrouded in a cloak of 'basicness'. There was nothing refined in pike fishing: it was simply a matter of chucking out a livebait whenever a pike made known its presence in the swim of a roach angler. Just occasionally the hapless pike would take the even more hapless roach, and would be hauled without ceremony into the bank and most likely killed for its trouble. Few pike ever had the chance to learn by their experience. Few anglers ventured out in the winter months: pike angling was only regarded as a winter sport and then only by comparatively few anglers. The combination of these and other factors meant that not a great deal of advance was made over the years. While would-be pike anglers were catching enough fish to keep them happy, in a low-key way, there was not the call to improve the situation.

Martin Gay tackling up, just after dawn

Pike were never caught in large numbers and few anglers were especially bothered. It was not until some successful pike anglers showed the general angling public what the species had to offer and demonstrated that they could expect not just the odd pike every few outings but several big and hard fighting fish per day, that their interest was aroused. By about 1960 an increasing number of anglers had learned that far from being a winter-only species, pike could be caught regularly in the summer, providing superb sport in the process.

There is a distinct correlation between success with pike and what we are able to learn from their capture. Anglers of yesteryear, who in general caught few pike, and then usually in specific circumstances only, easily formed what were actually preconceived ideas about the species, and only extensive fishing more recently has proved and disproved early ideas. As recently as twenty-five years ago it was a commonly held view that pike were poorly conditioned fish in the summer months, that they took a longer time than any other species of coarse fish to recover from spawning (despite the fact that they are also the earliest coarse fish to spawn) and that they should be left alone until October. Most river boards (as they were titled until the 1970s) substantiated this view by making it illegal to fish for pike until the autumn. To compound this further, many anglers actually objected to others summer pike fishing because such activities could spoil their own fishing. Summer pike enthusiasts were very thin on the ground throughout the 1960–75 period, although some pike angling was carried out on the Norfolk Broads, waters throughout Scotland and Ireland, and, occasionally, on quiet waters in England.

As our knowledge of pike improved, so did the numbers of pike caught to complement it. As more pike were caught so did our knowledge improve. Those (relatively few) of us who were piking with some success in the 1960s caught pike from areas in numbers, in certain cases, and failed to catch pike from other areas without knowing why. It became clear from fairly extensive fishing that pike favoured particular spots, but it took Ray Webb and Barrie Rickards, in 1970, to define this phenomenon and give it a name – in effect, 'hotspots' were born. Today, just about every pike angler in the country knows what hotspots are and spends a lot of time trying to find them.

From about 1965, and for the next decade, the angling 'divisions' of carp fishing and bass fishing were both independently undergoing something of a revolution in their choice of tackle. Richard Walker and his friends within the 'Carp Catchers Club' had shown the angling public that carp could be caught by design. Clive Gammon, among others, had shown that bass were a sporting fish to be enjoyed from beach and rocky ledge. But tackle was a limiting factor in both cases in so far as properly designed rods, good line and reliable hooks were not freely available. Just as science was progressing with all manner of

Martin Gay and Barrie Rickards pulling a magic lure from the hat – taking time out to discuss things on a lure-fishing day on a Fenland drain

improvements to modern living, so improved resins, and glass-fibre cloth, polymer science and carbon steel were being upgraded to the benefit of anglers. Better, lighter and longer rods made of phenolic resin-bonded glass; finer abrasion-resistant but stronger monofilament lines and strong hooks in smaller sizes all worked together at a time when anglers were both increasing in numbers *and* increasing their collective thirst for better fishing and knowledge.

Tackle developments improved across the full spectrum of coarse fishing interests. There can be no doubt that pike fishermen benefited the most from the rapidly developing tackle market. Casting baits or leads plus baits, which normally overload the rod, is a common practice among pike anglers. In the days of built cane rods, this frequently resulted in strains and sets in the material. Phenolic-resin glass, followed by quality carbon-fibre, effectively eliminated these problems, and these new materials improved casting and general tackle control (because of the lightness and the increased lengths of the rods) out of all proportion to that previously known. Thinner lines aided casting and better hooks aided the landing of fish, and so on. However, it was not so much the new-found benefits of the tackle that turned pike angling into a modern 'science' but anglers' thirst for the rediscovered fish, and the emergence of the understanding that in pike we had a species which could tax an anger's mind in just the same way as carp, barbel or perch.

As anglers began to understand pike, more details of their feeding habits and 'shoaling' activities became evident. It took many years, but with an increasingly supportive band of anglers it became appreciated that pike fed, for the most part at least, within clearly defined feeding bands on most days. These feeding spells, which would often start by the clock and end just as abruptly, last for several weeks at a time and at the same time each year, but can vary from water to water. As the evidence became clearer so it could be demonstrated that pike were not gluttons that fed at any time and just whenever food passed them by, but were especially finicky in their habits. Demonstrably pike are creatures of habit, yet there can be occasions when normal habits are abandoned.

On certain waters only, and almost always during the months between December and March, the fry of such species as roach and bream will gather in enormous numbers in small areas (usually just one area per water) and provide rich and very easy pickings for the pike, week in, week out. We still do not understand why the small fry – usually the current year's spawning of 1–3in – gather like this, but it comes as no surprise to find large numbers of pike in residence within days of it happening.

This kind of frenzied feeding, so often seen for these short periods each winter, might belie the belief that pike are nothing more than opportunist feeders, but such is not the case, and these occurrences are very special, short-lived and found on only a few waters. Twenty-five years ago very little was known about fry-feeding pike, and, I suspect, for the most part not even acknowledged as a phenomenon. Today, thanks to an interchange of ideas – albeit on a still limited scale – we know how to fish for these pike, the feeding habits of which change for the duration of the fry-gathering. The fact that it occurs almost entirely when the water temperatures are at their lowest may have something to do with it, but so could light levels and day length.

The twenty-year period from the mid-1950s saw an appreciable resistance within the ranks of sometime pike anglers to the idea that there was, in effect, a science of pike fishing. The long-held practice of hurling out a bung, supporting a livebait impaled on large hooks still continues to this day, but it is a practice rarely seen and this is due entirely to the better communication between pike anglers and the universal desire to catch more fish.

A combination of these two factors, or at least the acceptance of the need for better communication, gave rise to the birth of the Pike Society, and latterly to the improved and renamed Pike Anglers' Club. This organisation, which has been foremost in the fight to protect the species and to provide a mouthpiece for pike anglers across all factions within coarse and game angling, saw the need to protect pike not only from the activities of pike angling but, at least as important, from the destruction of habitat. Pike need a co-ordinated survival plan in order to protect them from anglers because, as we have learned by bitter experience, they do not take kindly to repeated capture, nor to bad handling. Education has been high on the priority list of the PAC throughout its active existence and will continue to be so well into the future.

The past twenty years have seen a radical change in angling attitudes towards the species and the practical side of fishing for them, but undoubtedly the future will see a greater need directed towards the problems of environmental protection. Without clean water and healthy fish stocks, there will be no pike to fish for. Pike, being the predator at the top of the freshwater food chain, stand the greatest risk of catastrophe, and if we are able to protect pike, then all species beneath it are assured of a healthy future.

The Pike Anglers' Club must take much of the credit for the improving attitude of anglers in general towards pike, but so can a number of individuals, including the authors of this book. As we fished our way through the 1980s, however, we arrived at what may be called 'the chicken and egg situation'. As more anglers discovered the pleasures of pike angling, caught more and bigger pike, so more encouraging reports of good fish were published in the weekly angling press and more in-depth articles were published in the monthly magazines. Not surprisingly, this encouraged and attracted more anglers into pike fishing, thereby increasing the pressure on pike and pike waters – not always to the benefit of the pike themselves.

Whatever has been stated about pike in the past, they are not a particularly robust species (unlike carp, for example) and must be treated respectfully when caught. Inexperienced anglers are frequently ill-equipped to speedily and efficiently unhook pike and frequently handle the fish poorly on the bank. The combination of these two problems alone have often caused the demise of a pike fishery without the anglers ever knowing what they have done wrong. Pike caught, even frequently, by experienced anglers mostly survive to thrive and grow, and show no ill-effects by this treatment, but keeping pike out of water for more than a few moments and allowing them to thrash about on the bank, or in a boat, unrestrained, is potentially fatally damaging. We have recently timed anglers on film keeping big pike out of the water for in excess of five minutes, which is totally unacceptable. Pike which are deeply hooked (usually caused by inattentiveness and poor bite indication), frequently meet the same fate, *especially* if the angler has spent some time ineffectively prodding about with a disgorger. The heart of the pike is situated only a short way back from the throat and close to the gullet, so large hooks can pierce the gut-wall and the heart without the angler knowing that he has done so. It is important to note that this is especially true of barbless hooks.

These are just some of the problems addressed by the PAC, and others, in recent years, but progress is being made. However, we are close to reaching the stage of saturation fishing on certain of the known big-fish waters, and we should be addressing this and associated problems now, while there is still much we can do. The last thing anyone wishes is for the effects of overfishing to work against the sport, thereby diminishing the numbers of serious pikers, with the inevitable retrograde steps that would follow.

Having too few quality pike fisheries leads to overcrowding, with the result that there is a gradual increase in pike mortality and a tailing away of interest.

One way to overcome the problem is to create put-and-take fisheries; indeed, a few resourceful fisheries managers are attempting this with some degree of success. Basicaly, all that is required is an existing fishery with a viable stock of cyprinids (food stock fish) and a replenishable number of pike. A syndicate, or day-ticket fishery is formed, while the fishery manager carefully monitors the catches of pike and weighs up the likelihood of pike deaths, or removals, and thereby replaces pike for pike as the need arises. As a result of the unenlightened attitude of some trout water managers, unwanted pike are regularly offered on the open market, and these are used for restocking purposes. If a twenty-pounder dies, it is simply replaced and the anglers remain happy. If the predator/prey ratio becomes imbalanced, the recourse is to stock with further cyprinids and/or to regularly discharge into the water sufficient numbers of stock-size trout or even deadbaits. Some fisheries have been running for years like this, and in certain cases the (stocked) pike have been known even to increase in weight for limited periods. More usually, they manage to maintain their weight or lose a little while they settle down. Much depends upon the type of water from which the pike were initially transferred and, to a degree, the quality of the water into which they have been moved.

This system is nothing if not artifical, but the situation satisfies many anglers, several of whom have achieved personal bests from just such fisheries. It is easy enough to be scathing of this approach, but that is not the purpose of this discussion, and in any case for this style of fishery management it is for the individual to decide whether or not it suits him or her. Additionally, we have collectively learned no small amount of information regarding the dietary requirements of pike from these carefully controlled fisheries.

The one general category of fishery in which pike stand little chance of reaching an old age unmolested is the trout reservoir. It appears that few fisheries managers of trout waters have any sympathy for pike nor any understanding of pike angling or the role that pike play in a well-balanced fishery. As a result, pike in most of these waters are pilloried from the day that they are born and an attempt is made to eradicate them because they eat trout. The fact that pike eat far more coarse fish than trout, which can be clearly demonstrated, escapes attention. It is coarse fish such as roach and perch that compete directly for food with trout, not the pike. Removing pike from any water almost always results in an increased tonnage of smaller pike, which predate more heavily on whatever food stocks there are, be that trout or coarse fish. This is a proven fact, and it shows clearly that such pike removal exercises are a waste of money and manpower. But most fisheries managers know this in their hearts, what they are actually demonstrating is a prejudice against pike.

The finest predator of pike is another, bigger pike, and this is the case for only one reason – the pike has evolved into the role it occupies today. No predator eats itself out of existence.

The relatively few trout reservoirs that have opened up, sometimes for very limited periods, such as Blythefield, Weirwood, Ardingley, Grafham, Rutland, Bewlbridge and Llandegfedd have all, and without exception, provided pike angling of the highest quality. Each of these waters is rich in its ecology and was allowed to develop in its formative years without man's interference. It thus becomes an inevitable fact that good pike fishing was to follow, given only the required access. No harm whatsoever has come to the fisheries in the meantime, nor to the other species contained within them, whether trout or coarse fish.

In order to achieve good fish well into the future, anglers first and foremost need to safeguard the fishing we have at present. There can be little doubt that within the last decade or so pike angling in Britain has been as productive as at any period in its history. Everything came together – our knowledge of the species, and the quality of the fishing and its availability – and that is not likely to be repeated. The reason for this is twofold: first, there are too many pike anglers, and pike do not take too kindly to repeated capture, to bad handling and to deep hooking (and all of these factors are still common). Secondly, environmental pressure by way of human development and (human)

Martin Gay bending into a big pike on a Fenland river

derived pollution are both working against the long-term survival of quality fisheries. The boom years of the 1950s and 1960s which saw the excavation of numerous gravel pits, bore fruit twenty years later by way of rich and productive fisheries. The pike benefited as much as any species. Thirty years ago, our rivers were, in general, clean and reasonably free of chemical pollution. Eutrophication was a word found only in the biological dictionaries. The productivity of reservoirs and lochs as pike fisheries was yet to be discovered. Which left us with the Norfolk Broadland, the Fens of Cambridgeshire/Norfolk, Kent/Sussex, and Somerset. Angling pressure on these areas was so low that common knowledge about them did not matter. Therein lies the key to the safeguarding of our existing pike fisheries. In a sentence, 'Keep pike angling pressure well under control'.

Consequently, we need to look for properly managed pike fishing which keeps a check on catches and the quality of angling skills, and which will close down fisheries temporarily if the angling pressure becomes too high. But for this to be achieved in any meaningful way waters will need to be run on a syndicated basis. And the costs of fishery ownership, or long-term leases, are prohibitive if there is the slightest chance that members may be prevented from fishing 'their' water for a period of some weeks at a time. Human nature being what it is, good fishing will not be ignored and it takes a strong will to limit fishing to two or three days per month, which on the one hand will amost certainly safeguard the future sport, but on the other deprives the angler of the very reason that he or she goes fishing.

Limited access to pike fisheries is the *only* way to maintain quality fishing. Limited access can mean: opening the water for only a few days each week/month/year, keeping the number of anglers very low and/or each of these things, as well as setting up prohibited areas within the fishery. This means keeping anglers completely away from large areas of the water for all time. One area which could easily fit this is the spawning site. We know nowadays that some time during late December until the season ends on 14 March, at least one area within most fisheries, and sometimes more, are frequented by spawning gatherings of pike. It would be a simple matter to shut that part of the water down from, say, 20 December each year. On some waters where almost all the pike gather in this (or these) areas, this procedure would give these pike a rest-from-angling spell of about six months and at a time when they can be highly vulnerable. Such arguments are not restricted to preserving pike fishing, but might be more widely applied.

A second period of the season when pike are even more vulnerable to angling pressure is in the summer. This is a converse statement because during the summer pike are at their most 'game', fight best and look tremendous. But that is the very problem – they fight too well and feed voraciously, and it is not a good time to put them under pressure. I have now reached the decision that I will not fish for pike during the summer, and I am of the opinion that on popular fisheries especially, summer piking should no longer be permitted, and where the demand from anglers is such that they want continued summer piking it should be allowed with lures only. Livebaiting and deadbaiting in the summer months results in too many deeply hooked fish (because they feed much more voraciously than when the water is cold) and fish which recover too slowly (or not at all) after a prolonged battle and find it difficult to regain their strength.

Another way to safeguard the sport into the future is the maintenance of 'artificial' waters. This can be achieved either by adopting the 'put-and-take' management ideas of simply replacing with fresh pike all those assumed to be dead, as the need arises; or (and this approach is adopted with a great deal of success by Neville Fickling on waters under his control) by insisting on a high standard of pike angling and handling techniques, by feeding the pike with deadbaits in quantity, and/or by stocking with food fish. This may be done to maintain what would otherwise be an artificially high pike/prey fish balance. It can work well, but as an angler you have to decide which approach suits you.

Martin Gay with a nicely shaped pike

Personally, I am not interested in either approach, but if the former ever became the norm I would immediately stop piking – I could live with the second way, but it would not be long before I lost interest in piking.

A better and far more natural way to maintain good pike fishing is, on the one hand, to adopt the restricted access ideals and to apply them to good quality, general fisheries, which can then be maintained to suit all angling interests. With this approach many golden opportunities are even now being missed on our 'trout' reservoirs because opposing interests cannot meet midway. In general terms, trout reservoirs in Britain are clean and productive fisheries, the waters breeding many coarse fish species, among them pike, to a large size and biomass. Unfortunately, and through a combination of factors, not least of which is the fact that coarse anglers will not pay trout angling prices to get access to these commercially run waters, and that trout anglers will not tolerate other anglers on their waters, the potential of these waters goes largely wasted. Meanwhile, the coarse fish are persecuted unnecessarily and wantonly. One day we might come to our senses and start to share our resources equally. In the meantime, the pike fishing potential for Great Britain will begin to decline from its elevated status of being among the finest to an also-ran. And we will have only ourselves to blame.

There is plenty of time to stop this happening and I have highlighted a few of those ways within these pages. We need to revise our attitudes towards our future sport – we have the best tackle and the finest techniques available to anyone, better than at any time in history. These very facts can so easily be the undoing of pike waters, but for the realisation and the acceptance that we *still* need to manage our waters correctly. We are still not doing this in the way that we should, but we must.

9

THE DEVELOPMENT OF PIKING

That pike angling has a long history will be obvious to a newcomer from the moment he picks up a book and begins to browse. Few areas of angling have such a rich heritage of myth, legend, and, indeed, factual basis. The pike itself has a much longer history on Earth than human beings: *Esox lucius* has had to survive the human predator for about the last three or four million years of Earth history, yet for over 80 million years the genus *Esox* has been around. Gay and Rickards (1989) argue that species of the genus became separated into North American and European stocks when the Atlantic Ocean first opened and began to spread. The European line of evolution faltered at about 25 million years ago but the North American line continued from *E. tiemani* to the muskellunge and hence to the pickerels and (Northern) pike, the last, *our* pike, travelling by the Bering Land Bridge to reach Europe from North America, and not the other way round as usually supposed. That's why we have only *one* pike, whereas in North America they still have several (with their 'geological' tendency to prefer slightly warmer conditions south of the circumpolar distribution of our own pike).

This is then the scene that was set round about the time of the Ice Age and somewhat earlier, when humans first came into contact with the marauding predator. Naturally, our records of this are restricted to archaeological sites where pike bones occur in association with human artifacts. Some of the pike sizes calculated by Russian archaeologists, from the remains of vertebrae, are utterly ludicrous – up to 100lb judging from the estimated fish length. When the pike really began to get into European consciousness and literature, the record is still very sparse but has been well documented by Hoffman (*in* Crossman and Casselman, 1987) in what he defines as a period of *protohistory*, that is before historical records were well kept. What is quite clear is that the pike had an unenviable reputation even in these dim and distant times, and it is equally obvious to me that fear was the prime cause of the more ridiculous myths, such as pike eating dogs and children, attacking horses and so on.

Against this backdrop, the modern misconceptions of the pike as an avid bird eater do rather pale into insignificance. Not, I hasten to add, that the modern scientists have much to be proud of in this respect, as the above claims by archaeologists testify. Nor were anglers much better, with totally unbelievable claims for 90lb fish from Ireland, against the 'smaller' equally unlikely captures. I would like to believe that a 60lb pike has been caught: but I do not believe that it has – 50lb, yes. The general public, too, gets almost as carried away with pike as it does with dinosaurs. The more discreditable stories are outlined by Rickards (1986) but I must mention one that surfaced once again in 1988 – that a Russian pike ate a small child, rescued alive by his father when the pike was cut open! Quite what the child used for air during this lengthy process is not discussed.

The development of pike angling proper took place, then, alongside all this inherited debris of myth and suspicion, fear and castigation, and it is hardly likely that the sport would develop very quickly. Despite its long history it has developed only slowly. Some years ago, I and my friend Malcolm Bannister decided to investigate thoroughly the published literature on pike angling. One of our objectives was to try to determine who was responsible for which technique and when the technique was developed. We also made a decision not to deal with the modern angler (1960s to 1990s) because that would form a subject of a new, different study, and so we ended our story just into the 1950s when one or two classic and most important books were published (see Rickards and Bannister, 1991).

This work was certainly a voyage of discovery and surprise. Instead of the large number of innovative works we expected, we found very few. Pike were mostly dealt with by game fishermen, often as a single chapter in books on salmon and trout. While these books were instructive enough, they were, in fact, simply repeating, recording and rewriting earlier discoveries; rarely did they add much that was new. (Remember that we are talking about a period of time from 1496 to 1951 – almost 500 years.)

One or two of the problems we faced were interesting, such as appraising the (anonymous) pamphlet added in 1496 to Dame Juliana Berners' work on heraldry, and judging Izaak Walton's contribution to pike angling. Walton said very little about pike angling, and it did not read, unlike most of *The Compleat Angler* (which first appeared in 1653), as first-hand experience should read. There was nothing new in Walton except possibly his use of line clips (which were reinvented in the 1980s, although dealt with in crude form by Richard Walker in the 1960s). In many other respects, of course, the May 1653 edition of *The Compleat Angler* was a milestone in angling history.

In contrast, Berners' work was innovative: it was, after all, the first work to be written on angling. The problem is that we have no idea who the author was. Furthermore, so much useful information is distilled into a few pages that it is clear that pike angling must have had a long history. It is not unreasonable to suppose that pike angling dates back to the twelfth and thirteenth centuries when it took place in stew ponds; certainly, pike, as well as eels and cyprinids, were a product of such ponds, and catching pike on rod and line or, at least, on (long) line, would have been an efficient way of doing so.

We discovered that, over a period of almost five hundred years (1682–1951), there were only ten innovative contributors to the development of pike angling, excluding Berners and Walton: Robert Nobbes; Cholmondely Pennell; John Bickerdyke; Alfred Jardine; William Senior; J.W. Martin; Edward Spence; Sidney Spencer; Norman Hill and Charles Thurlow-Craig.

We also discovered that almost all piking techniques, including those which we describe in this book, were established a very long time ago. They were often forgotten, or out of favour for some reason, or simply not appreciated by the ordinary angler, and then they were reinvented, perhaps finding a readier acceptance in a different climate of opinion or leisure. On making a list of all the basic tackle, techniques and approaches, and noting their first appearance in the written record, we found that by 1896 no less than 82 per cent of the major discoveries had been made. The only discoveries which I can say were made this century were: fly-fishing for pike and Fred J. Taylor-style wobbled deadbaiting (by William Senior in 1900); Trent Otter spinning flight (by J.W. Martin=Trent Otter, 1907); twitched deadbaits, mackerel deadbaits and drifter rigs (by Spence, 1928); American lure-fishing techniques (by Spencer, 1936); modern conservation techniques, *pars* (by Hill and Craig in the 1940s).

But to return to Berners, it is a fascinating fact that herring deadbaits were used in the fifteenth century. We do not know how they used their herrings in those days, whether they were salted, frozen or dried. And with the difficulties of travel, the thought of a fifteenth-century angler travelling from Wisbech or King's Lynn to Morton's Leam (which was already built in the Fens) with dead fish as bait for pike, is captivating. They would have deserved their pike. And if the pike was only for food why did they not simply eat the herring? No, this was pike fishing for the sake of pike fishing, with food as a bonus if they were successful.

Berners also used static deadbaits, attractor scents, threaded traces and a sunken float rig. I remember Ray Webb reinventing threaded traces in the 1950s, although many had done it before him. On careful reading of Berners, the sunken float rig is not the same as the one used today; in fact, the method described in the pamphlet might have lifted the herring off the bottom, or it might have merely made it slightly buoyant. The sunken float rig was not used again, as far as I am aware, until Norman Hill described it in 1944. Today it is very popular. The Berners' pamphlet also describes free-line rigs, ledger fishing (possibly with livebaits) and the use of dyed lines, but possibly not the use of fixed leads on the line. By any measure, fifteenth-century piking must have been reasonably sophisticated, despite inadequacies of line, rods and equipment in general.

Less than one hundred years later, *The Compleat Angler* mentions fixed

A less frequent sight these days: a pike thrown on the bank of a northern reservoir to rot away

leads, wire traces (specifically, not by implication only), spun deadbaits, ledgered livebaits, gorge fishing and sink-and-draw fishing. The last was not carried out as we do it today, in the sense that the deadbait was retrieved tail first. I wish that I could feel easy about attributing these inventions to Walton, but I cannot. I am sure they were developments made by keen pike anglers between Berners and Walton. A clue to this theory is the anonymous booklet of 1577 entitled *The Arte of Angling*.

Thus Nobbes (1682) becomes the first of the innovators. Though his discoveries are few in number, all his writing breathes direct, first-hand experience: feeding patterns (largely ignored until today); 'Bellars'-style hooks (which were not used again until the 1960s by Vic Bellars); half-baits; artificial lures and two – that is, consecutive – wire traces.

With Pennell, Bickerdyke and Jardine we move into early modern piking. Their books read well today, and between them they were responsible for almost half the discoveries that make up piking as we know it. Pennell invented his own tackle rigs, and not only in pike fishing. He studied growth rates; practised modern spinning; outlawed the use of the eye-socket grip, and detected on-the-spot-feeding. Bickerdyke, another very practical man, was responsible for the Gazette bung (which is still with us, sadly); noted that single strand wire kinks; used eels and smelt for deadbait; detected 'shoaling' of pike, and used adjustable Ryder hooks and advanced paternoster tackle. Jardine is famous for his snap tackle and also invented the butt ring floatant dispenser.

Jardine brought to pike fishing for the first time in its history, a professional approach and, unlike all the innovators before him, he caught big fish. He was one of the most successful pike anglers in history in terms of big fish caught. And, like later big fish captors, controversy followed him. There is certainly more than an element of doubt about some of his fish, regarding either their capture or their weight.

Modern anglers owe a great debt to the past, to the innovators whose discoveries have been outlined. Around 80 per cent of what we do was done by them first, with inferior tackle, with inadequate transport, and with inadequate clothing for an essentially winter pursuit.

In modern times, pride of place must go to the development of static deadbaiting by Fred J. Taylor, and others to a lesser degree, in the 1950s. Remember that this was described by Berners in 1496, but since Pennell in the 1860s it had been completely missed by all the innovative pikers. Even Norman Hill whose chapters published in 1944 were possibly the most modern ever written, completely missed the use of static deadbaits. Hill's son David confirmed that his father considered that a bait should move for pike, even if very slowly. So enormous credit must go to the redevelopers of the static deadbait technique. And it is worth noting that it really did transform pike fishing in this country, making it easily available to anyone without the difficulty many would have of obtaining livebaits – for example, dwellers in the centres of large conurbations – and without the undoubted costs of lure fishing.

Another developing facet of pike angling in the 1950s, one which dominated, and effectively suppressed Thurlow-Craig's movement towards a world of lure anglers, was Dennis Pye and his livebaiting techniques of the Norfolk Broads. I should really say 'technique', for that is all it was: the use of a large livebait, free-swimming save for a float, in shallow water closely adjacent to the Norfolk reed-beds. Lure fishing, in the form of trolling, did continue in Ireland (as always) and in Norfolk with the Vincents, both father and son. And deadbait fishing continued with Bill Giles and Reg Sandys who developed rigs. But Dennis Pye stole the headlines and became the first real catcher of big pike since Alfred Jardine. Like Jardine before him, and others since, his catches became controversial, and I do find some of the claims disturbing. Having said that, it must also be asserted that Dennis Pye's contribution to pike angling, in inspiring would-be pike anglers, was considerable and on a par at that time with the importance of Fred J. Taylor's innovations.

The Montgomery Canal in Shropshire where the legendary Thurlow-Craig learned the art of plug fishing

Eventually, the static deadbait method of fishing overtook the Pye method, because it had a more universal application. Even if the baits themselves were available, the Pye technique does not often work, except in identical circumstances to those met with on the Norfolk Broads. The deadbaiting approach, on the other hand, works both there and in many other types of water.

However, the previous paragraph oversimplifies the demise of the Pye philosophy. Contributory factors included the development of totally new live and deadbaiting techniques which Ray Webb and I elucidated in 1971 *(Fishing for Big Pike)*, but which had been arrived at independently by anglers in different parts of the country, on quite different waters. Very notable among these was Dave Steuart, but also others like Trevor Housby and Peter Wheat. Strangely enough, the livebaiting improvements had already been carried out by Norman Hill, but everyone had overlooked his book. Steuart continued successfully, but with modified rigs, the Pye concept of a big livebait for a large pike; but ultimately this whole approach faded as anglers opted for smaller baits, both on the grounds of conservation and of efficiency.

Meanwhile, Taylor's deadbait rigs and tactics were being improved out of all recognition; and deadbaiting today is a refined art, properly done with excellent hooking systems, completely new landing and *un*hooking systems, and a totally new concept of pike conservation and the role of the species in natural systems. The 1970s and 1980s really did see great strides in pike angling, perhaps the greatest since Berners and Nobbes. All this was helped by the arrival of new materials – carbon, electronics, net-making material, and so on, but the developments themselves have been fundamental.

One thread I have left until last, and that is lure fishing. This aspect of piking has never really caught the full imagination of pikers. Spence, Spencer, and then Hill and Thurlow-Craig, lit the touch-paper, but the result was a damp squib which spluttered fitfully in the 1960s, before being fully eclipsed by the new deadbaiting techniques. With both deadbaiting and livebaiting currently on a technical acme, the lure-fishing approach is once again poised to take off, this time as an *alternative* to baits; one of the reasons for its failure in the past has been the tendency of fanatics to try to sell it as the *only* way to pike fish, or the only sporting way, or the most successful way – all demonstrably false claims to anyone who is a generalist. But lure fishing has become a boom interest and a boom business. In the late 1980s it was perhaps realised for the first time, by anglers in general, just how successful the method could be. So lure fishing could be a bubble that will burst, or it could be the new face of pike angling into the year 2000. If so, then I hope it will be accompanied by burgeoning developments in bait fishing.

This chapter would not be complete if I did not mention the works of an old friend, Fred Buller who has studied the lore of pike and pike angling as no one else. The testaments to his efforts are recorded in two inspiring books: *Pike* and *The Domesday Book of Pike* (see Bibliography). *Pike* faithfully records all the techniques that have been used down the years, and the ideas that accompanied them. *The Domesday Book*, as it is usually termed, lists all the claimed pike of more than 35lb. It proves that some claims are false; yet others in the book have been shown to be fakes since the book was published. There is impressive documentation of fish up to 50lb or so. Thereafter, the documentation is rather unconvincing and I have never been convinced by the fish of 60, 70 and 90lb that are included. Since that book, others have listed additional pike of 90lb. I don't believe those either. There are few of 80lb incidently (in fact, I cannot recall one as I write). Why? Because 90lb isn't quite such a big lie as 100lb, but it sounds nearly there! An 80lb lie would be pointless. I have written elsewhere on this subject so will not pursue it further, except to say that none of this detracts from Fred Buller's work which is a mighty service to pikers: even if it includes the warts, we need to know that too. And it encapsulates all that is pike angling, from its inherited myths and fearfulness, to the fakes and charlatans that are with us even today. Out of this the innovations will come, the truths will be recognised and perhaps that rather exclusive list of a dozen or so anglers will be added to. Time will tell.

REFERENCES

Berners, S. *A Treatyse of Fysshynge wyth an Angle* (1496)

Bickerdyke, J. *Angling for Pike* (The Bazaar, Exchange & Mart Ltd, 1888)

Crossman, E.J. & Casselmann, J.M. *An Annotated Bibliography of the Pike, Esox lucius (Osteichthyes: Salmoniformes)* (Royal Ontario Museum, 1987)

Gay, M. & Rickards, R.B. *Pike* (Boydell & Brewer, 1989)

Hill, N. *A Fisherman's Recollections* (Herbert Jenkins Ltd, 1944)

Hoffman, R. (see Crossman & Cassellmann, 1987)

Jardine, A. *Pike and Perch* (George Routledge & Sons Ltd, 1896)

Martin, J.W. *Pike and Perch Fishing* (W. Brendan & Son Ltd, 1907)

Nobbes, R. *The Compleat Troller* (1682)

Pennell, C. *The Book of the Pike* (1865)

Rickards, R.B. *Big Pike* (A. & C. Black, 1986)

Rickards, R.B. & Bannister, M. *The Ten Greatest Pike Anglers* (Boydell & Brewer, 1991)

Rickards, R.B. & Fickling, N. *Zander* (2nd edition) (Boydell & Brewer, 1990)

Senior, W. *Pike and Perch* (Longmans, Green & Co, 1990)

Sidley, J. *River Piking* (Boydell & Brewer, 1987)

Spence, E.F. *The Pike Fisher* (A. & C. Black, 1928)

Spencer, S. *Pike on the Plug* (H.F. & G. Witherby, 1936)

Thurlow-Craig, C. *Spinner's Delight* (Hutchinson's Library of Sports & Pastimes, 1951)

Walton, I. *The Compleat Angler* (1653)

Webb, R. & Rickards, R.B. *Fishing for Big Pike* (A. & C. Black, 1971)

INDEX

INDEX